Firecracker Frolic

Hilarious Tales of a Mischievous Kid

***

By

Anita S. Sridharan

First published by AuthorHouse 05/17/04

ISBN: 1-4184-0185-4 (e-book)
ISBN: 1-4184-0186-2 (Paperback)
Library of Congress Control Number:
2004092336

Printed in the United States of America
Bloomington, Indiana

This book is printed on acid free paper.

This book is dedicated to
my loving husband,
the man who keeps the twinkle
in my eyes.

Contents

Introduction

"Firecracker Frolic" is a rollicking romp through the childhood of four outlandishly mischievous preacher's kids. No one is safe from their playful antics and elaborate schemes. Everyone takes a turn in the hot seat.

Everything that you are about to read is absolutely true. I know. I was there! I am the youngest little firecracker of the four.

It is my sincere wish that you laugh out loud at the merry devilment and imaginative plots contained within these pages.

Relax, put your feet up, and enjoy "Firecracker Frolic."

"Answer me, O Lord, out of the goodness of your love;
in your great mercy turn to me.
Do not hide your face from your servant; answer me quickly,
for I am in trouble."

Psalms 69:16-17

N.I.V.

x

Chapter One

Southern Discipline

My parents were dubiously blessed with four little firecrackers that popped off, with a bang, in every direction.

Restraining exploding firecrackers is a tricky business. That is especially true when they are detonating simultaneously. One is thrust into a frantic dash here, there, and everywhere to halt ignitions and extinguish flames.

Mamma always swore that we would be the death of her. It is amazing that we were not the death of each other and ourselves. We were creative, mischievous, and absolutely fearless. We concocted and carried out elaborate schemes on a regular basis. As a result, we were in the hot seat a lot.

We always knew how much trouble we were in by the way mamma called us. One name meant come here. Two names meant you're in big trouble. Three names meant prepare to meet your maker.

When summoned with multiple titles, our minds raced through a list of possibilities as our legs did the quick trot to find her. "Anita Susan!" gave me the shivers.

We never volunteered information during these confrontations. It was best to stay quiet and see exactly how much she knew. The very last thing we wanted to do was begin a blabbering apology for an undiscovered offense or add tidbits of information that may have escaped her notice.

Corrective action was swift and sure. We were held accountable for our misdeeds and were expected to make amends.

We were not stupid. Subterfuge and evasion became a way of life. We knew it was always better to get away with something if we could. Punishment was not fun.

When it came to discipline, or anything else for that matter, divide and conquer was never a game that we could play with our folks. What one said, the other enforced. They stuck together like bark to a tree. Our adz lay disused and rusted. Some things were not worth effort of trying.

Our parents employed a variety of methods when dealing with conflict. "Kiss and make up" was the method we despised above all others.

Imagine the appearance of two fighting cats. Have you got it? Now, imagine pulling them apart, holding them face to face, and ordering them to make up. Yeah, right! The results are predictable.

It was, exactly, the same way with us. We kissed, hugged, and said we were sorry, "nicely." The real show began when mamma walked away.

We dramatically wiped away the kiss with the backs of our hands. Then, we stuck our thumbs in our ears and wiggled our fingers, crossed our eyes, and stuck out our tongues. A whispered retraction, a punch or a pinch, and a

final thrust of tongues concluded the
performance.

Sticking out ones tongue was strictly against
the rules. Another round of "kiss and make
up" invariably followed if we were caught.
That was the very *last* thing we wanted. These
were top secret operations that were covertly
practiced when the coast was clear.

Another remedy, for bad behavior, involved
plopping us onto the sofa. We were instructed
to sit there, think about what we had done, and
call when we were ready to apologize.
Sometimes, that took a little while; sometimes,
it took the better part of an afternoon.

At first, we sat with crossed arms and fumed
over our incarceration. After that, we
vigorously engaged in self-justification and
blaming of others. Then, we reflected on
whether or not we were truly remorseful for
our actions or would apologize just to get off
of the couch.

Mamma stopped by, from time to time, and
asked if we were ready to apologize. At times,

we were ready; at other times, we had not finished with fuming. Sooner or later, we said we were sorry.

Apologies were offered with the appearance of abject sincerity but were not always genuine. Those sessions *did* teach us to think about actions and consequences. They were not totally successful, but they had merit.

One day, when I was perched on the sofa, I heard a crash in the kitchen. Against orders, I jumped up and raced in to see what had happened.

Mamma was sitting on the floor, next to a bowl of chocolate cake batter that had fallen and splattered everywhere. Batter was on the ceiling, on the walls, on her clothes, and in her hair. Holding an apron over her face, she sat and cried. I felt sorry for her and helped clean up the mess.

It was the only time I ever got off of the sofa without an apology.

Swearing was the one transgression for which there was no excuse and no defense. I would like to shake the hand of the man who invented the concept of washing ones mouth out with soap. That would serve nicely as atonement for the swift kick to his shins that would precede it.

Of all the nasty tastes in the world, soap rules supreme. Its use is the ultimate cou de grâce. Thank goodness that potty mouths were rarely a problem at our house.

Last, but certainly not least, was the "good old-fashioned switching." We had a ligustrum hedge, in the back yard, that was prolific. It was the source and nature's own, unlimited supply of the dreaded switch.

That slender, stinging piece of vexation was intended to leave a real and lasting impression on our psyche. It succeeded. It didn't slow us down very much, but it did leave an impression.

Fran, Tommy, Jeanne, and I romped through days filled with a sense of adventure and an awareness of discipline.

We engaged in all activities with gusto. With our friends and with each other, we navigated our way through childhood full steam ahead.

Chapter Two

Meet "The Baby"

My status, as "the baby" firecracker, in no way diminished my ability to sizzle and pop. I popped inside and outside the boundaries of our home on a regular basis.

Our house was a "too small" world. To blink was to discover that I was gone. A rusty, red tricycle and my walk-o-mobile (legs) were my tickets to AWOL heaven.

Our family banked at First Federal. It was a small-town bank that was located about two miles from our house. Once a week, Daddy drove our blue-and-white Chevy to the teller's window and deposited a check. The teller slid out a receipt, for daddy, and a grape sucker, for me, in return. She was a nice lady!

One action-packed day, when I was a three-year-old, I had a nickel in my pocket and a hankering for a lollipop. The solution was simple. With anticipation and resolve, I powered my beat-up tricycle down to the bank and into the drive through.

The teller freaked and instructed me, repeatedly, to move out of the line of cars. Undeterred, I showed her my nickel and politely asked, "Can I please have a lollipop?" She slid one out in desperation. After thanking her, I cheerfully pedaled onto the sidewalk and headed for home.

The police caught up with me about two blocks away from the bank. After stowing my tricycle in the trunk, they put me in the back seat of the cruiser. Imagine that! I was going to ride in a real police car!

The policemen asked what I was doing, where I lived, and if my mother knew where I was. I nicely answered all of their questions and enthusiastically asked them to turn on the siren. They shook their heads and laughed. I asked about their guns and listened intently as they radioed in my AWOL status. Cool!

It's a good thing that I was able to give them directions to our house. Otherwise, daddy would have picked me up in the slammer.

After the police left, daddy's instruction was emphatic and clear, "Stay in the yard!" Humph!

Soon after that, two teenage boys found me climbing over a fence in an attempt to gain entry to the closed, municipal pool. They escorted me home. Actually, they pried my fingers and toes out the fence and carried me.

That scared mamma. She began to visualize all of the other, possible conclusions to that scenario. I was drowned; I was kidnapped; I was molested.

Mamma read a story to me, from the newspaper, about a little girl who had been kidnapped and killed. She stressed that I could *not* go running around all over the place because it was too dangerous.

From an early age, I was exceptionally skilled at selective hearing. I made a mental note of the danger and decided to be more careful on my little adventures. Nobody was going to snatch *me*!

Since nothing else had worked, Mamma came up with the bright idea of tying me to the clothesline. She took a long rope, tied one end to the clothesline, and the other end to the back of my romper. That way, I could run and play but could *not* run away.

My homebound status was well planned and short-lived. When she tied me up, I stood mute and motionless, for a moment, to analyze the situation. It would have been the simplest thing in the world to climb up the clothesline pole and untie myself, but I did not do that. No, I thought about it and became indignant. From my point of view, she had just staked me out like Rover, and I did not like it one little bit!

So, what *did* I do? I stood in one spot and screamed at the top of my lungs in righteous anger. I was absolutely furious! Mamma thought I would settle down, in a few minutes, and get on with the business of playing.

Mamma underestimated the potency of my fury.

Not only did I not settle down, the screaming began to attract the attention of the neighbors. Mamma knew that she was not hurting me but was not convinced that the neighbors would understand that. She untied me.

Ding, ding, and ding. Round one goes to Susie with a TKO.

Mamma's instruction was also crystal clear. She said, "You stay in this yard. Do you understand me?" I said, "Yes ma'am." Humph!

We had a 30-gallon, galvanized steel washtub in the back yard. That summer, it was my personal, pint-sized swimming pool that was defended against all comers. It was also a dandy baptistery.

My daddy was a preacher, and I had watched him baptize people at our church. The way I saw it, these people had gotten the devil in them, and that old devil had to be drowned so they could be good again. That helps explain what happened next.

Mamma took me out onto the front porch, one Saturday afternoon, for a summer hair cut. She said she needed to get that long hair off of my neck because it was too hot. I didn't want a haircut, and boy, I was mad.

There was a cowlick, right in the middle of my bangs, which caused the hair to stick straight out in every direction. We had to pink tape the bangs down to my forehead so they would dry flat.

Half an hour later, I arose from that chair with wet hair and a high temper.

While sulking in the back yard, our pet cat, Boots, had the misfortune of making an appearance. I decided to catch Boots and give him a haircut. After all, he had a lot of hair too; it was only fair.

He apparently disagreed and immediately turned into a hissing, hair-raised maniac. I just knew that that cat had gotten the devil in him.

There was only one solution. He must be baptized.

After securing a grip on this pint-sized bundle of fangs and fur, I proceeded to baptize him in the name of the Father, the Son, and the Holy Ghost. AMEN!

When I pulled him up and out of the water, that cat went ballistic. Looking at all the bloody scratches on my arms, I came to the conclusion that I had succeeded only in making the devil mad. So, I baptized him again.

Mother flew out of the house, to see what the ruckus was about, and I had two wild cats on my hands.

Soon, mamma wasn't the only one that was flying around. Mary Poppins exploded onto the big screen. I thought that soaring with an umbrella was the ultimate in cool.

Umbrella in hand, I set out on a mission. Now, how was I going to get up onto the roof?

Our TV antenna was attached to a pole that was anchored into the ground about a foot away from the house. Perfect! After scampering up the pole and onto the highest peak of the roof, I tested the wind and prepared to fly.

Holding the open umbrella high in the air, I ran, at breakneck speed, to the edge of the roof and jumped. I continued, at breakneck speed, all the way to the ground. OUCH!

Thoroughly disgusted, I folded that worthless contraption and limped away. Mary Poppins, in my opinion, was a crock. I lost all respect.

Cats and heights were of interest to me for some reason. I had heard that cats always landed on their feet. Wishing to prove or disprove that theory, I caught the neighbor's cat and climbed as high as possible up a chinaberry tree.

With a spinning motion, I launched her into the air and watched to see what would happen. She landed on her feet and held a grudge against me for the rest of her life. What a sissy!

The next mission was finding out how the radio worked. Mamma told me that radio waves traveled through the air and into the box. That was only part of the story. I wanted to know what was inside of the box. She did not have an answer.

Unfortunately, I took a screwdriver and disassembled daddy's radio into a thousand different pieces. I walked away with a satisfied curiosity and a red behind. Oh well, no pain, no gain. They can rejoice that I didn't start with the TV.

Despite the fact that I was mischievous, the old ladies in the neighborhood seemed to enjoy my company. They treated me to cookies, cupcakes, and pies. We looked at magazines and cut out paper dolls or read stories.

Mamma wondered why a four-year-old spent so much time with older ladies and asked me about it. I just liked their company. I had "grandmas" handy all of the time. They thought I was "sweet." I liked that.

A collage project led me to Mrs. Peden's front door in search of a picture of a bee. We looked through all of her magazines without success. Finally, she took a little pair of sewing scissors and clipped the picture of a bumblebee out of her encyclopedia.

When mamma saw it, she thought I had mutilated her book and called Mrs. Peden to verify my claim. I did not ask my friend to do it; she did it because she loved me.

Older people have always liked me. I'm not sure why. An elderly man once gave me a stack of old, dirty postcards. He thought I might like to color on them. Thanking him, I accepted the cards and pondered over what I should do with them.

I sold them for a nickel apiece, door-to-door, in the neighborhood. In one afternoon, I cleared $4.95, made a lot of new friends, and bought coloring books and crayons.

On one rather misguided adventure with the money, I walked to the neighborhood convenience store and conned the clerk into selling me a nickel cigar.

Mamma decided that, since I lied to get it, she would allow me to punish myself with the pleasure of smoking it. She thought that I would become deathly ill, throw up, and never touch another tobacco product as long as I lived.

Unfortunately, things did not go as planned. Again and again, I laughed, inhaled, and blew. Mamma told me to enjoy myself and inhale deeply. She encouraged me to blow lots and lots of smoke. I was not sure why she was being so good-natured about it. I thought this was supposed to be naughty. I smoked the whole thing and frisked off to play without so much as one green gill.

Mamma was chagrined. She called me back into the house and lectured. The understanding was that I should never do that again.

Potty training was another issue that brought unexpected results. Mamma gave me a little, wooden potty, explained the procedure, and sat me down with my "Little Golden Books." I was a quick study and soon mastered it.

There was just one problem. I couldn't be bothered with the inconvenience of running to the potty all of the time. I was too busy, and it was a lot easier to water the grass or wet my underpants. We went around and around over that.

Mamma finally got tired of it and stopped fixing me up with dry underwear. I eventually came to the conclusion that wet pants felt yucky and used the potty.

Chapter Three

Temper, Temper

Once upon a time, there was a little girl named Susie. One day, Susie's mommy sent her out to play on the cool, green grass, in a yard filled with sunshine, where flowers bloomed and bees buzzed. Her mommy said, "Stay in the yard, Susie."

Susie played with her dolls, tossed her balls, and lay in the cool, green grass to watch the clouds as they slowly drifted past.

Soon, Susie felt lonely. She heard other little children playing in a yard nearby. Oh, how she longed to join in and play, but she remembered her mommy's words. "Stay in the yard, Susie."

So, Susie played tea party with her little dishes and picked flowers to wear in her golden hair. She could hear the other children laugh and play and felt sad.

She walked to the edge of the yard and called to them, "Can you come and play with me?" They did not hear her.

Susie stood and watched them for a while and then sat down to pick at the grass and wish that she could play with someone. Just then, Sarah noticed her and said, "Susie, come on down and play."

Susie was so happy that she forgot her mommy's words and skipped out of the yard to join her friends.

When her mommy saw that Susie was gone, she began to look for her. She called, "Susie, Susie." Her mommy was angry that Susie had disobeyed her.

When she found Susie, she took her hand and led her home for a spanking. She told Susie that, as long as she lived in her house, she had to obey her rules.

Susie said, "OK. Then I will just run away from home!" Her mommy thought she was just upset and did not pay any attention. She said, "OK. You just do that."

Susie went straight to her room, packed her little pink suitcase, and ran away. She did not know where she was going, but she was going far away where little girls could do what they wanted to do and did not get spankings.

Susie made plans as she walked, all alone, by the road. She would stop and ask nice ladies for food when she was hungry. She would sleep under a tree when she was tired. She knew that God would keep her safe if she remembered her prayers.

When her mommy saw that Susie was missing, she was worried. She searched and shouted her name, but she could not find her. She called Susie's daddy on the telephone and asked him to come home and help her look.

Susie's daddy found her several miles down the road. She was still carrying her little, pink suitcase. Her daddy put her in the car and drove home with her.

Mommy was cross and began to scold Susie. Susie said, "Mommy, you *told* me I could do it!" There was nothing her mommy could say. It was true. So, she told Susie to never run away again.

The moral of the story is this. Never, and I mean never, tell a bright and tenacious child that she can do something, unless you mean it because she will.

Chapter Four

The Two Musketeers

Robbie was the little red-haired boy, next door, that married me at the age of three under a banana tree in the back yard.

My wedding ensemble was fashioned out of a white bath towel (that was bobby-pinned to my hair) and a red-and-white quilt (that was wrapped around my shoulders and secured with three clothespins in front).

Robbie was regally attired in a gold, paper crown from Burger King and a Superman cape that puffed out and fluttered in the breeze.

We pledged our eternal love for each other, and he gave me my first kiss. That kiss sealed his fate as my partner in crimes and sharer in punishments. We were the inseparable, dynamic duo and the two musketeers.

Sunday afternoons, in the South, were boring. After church and a big dinner, the grown-ups read the paper and took a nap. When you're too little to read, too old to take a nap, and left to your own devices, interesting situations develops.

Robbie and I paid a price for our "great Sunday afternoon lipstick disaster." We were bored and decided to channel our artistic abilities into the creation of a grand painting on an empty bedroom wall.

Our medium was bright red lipstick. We artfully painted the wall with two tubes of Avon's finest but were not yet satisfied.

With the stealth of stalking lions, we crept into my parent's bedroom and silently snatched, from the dresser, two pairs of mamma's white, Sunday gloves. We donned those gloves and proceeded to smear lipstick in circles and swirls all over the wall.

We giggled, with jubilant delight, over the majesty of our creation. The volume of our laughter increased as the size of our masterpiece grew. That was our fatal mistake and the undoing of our glorious plan. We woke mamma.

After blistering my behind, she handed both of us a rag, a can of Comet, and a bucket of hot water (how apropos). We scoured and cried, and scrubbed and cried, and scoured and scrubbed and cried.

When it became clear that the lipstick would never come off, she relented and asked daddy to take some leftover paint and obliterate our creation forever.

Mamma wasn't the only one to discover our dastardly deeds. One afternoon, while studying for a Sunday sermon, daddy heard clunk-giggle, clunk-giggle, and clunk-giggle.

Just imagine his astonishment at finding that we had emptied every tin can from the kitchen cabinets, removed the labels, and tossed them over the fence in the back yard.

Only on the rarest of occasions did daddy become truly angry. When he did, it was all hands on deck, and snap to attention. It made an impression. He didn't have to say much to anyone.

That was one time that daddy was not pleased. We could offer him no explanation for our behavior. It was merely something to do. He gave us something to do all right. After retrieving each and every can, Robbie was sent home, and I was banished to my room.

We had mystery meals for a couple of weeks. It was the gift that kept on giving.

One day, Robbie and I turned into a couple of scheming, little thieves. We didn't mean to be bad. It wasn't our intention to actually *steal* anything.

We watched a re-run of "Treasure Island" and immediately engaged in play as evil swashbucklers on a white-sailed ship in the Caribbean Sea.

With yellow bandanas tied to our heads, plastic swords in our hands, and a stuffed parrot scotch-taped and safety-pinned to Robbie's left shoulder, we embarked on a mission to fill an empty shoebox with treasure. Aye matey!

Among the many items collected were two, twenty-dollar bills from mamma's wallet, junk jewelry, and a handful of pennies from daddy's collection of "wheaties."

We buried our treasure in the crawlspace under the house, drew a map to this secret location, and found another game to play.

That night, after kisses and prayers, I snuggled under the covers to sleep. It hit like a bolt of lightening. Jumpin' Jehoshaphat! I hadn't put the money back! Mamma was going to *kill* me!

In a state of panic, I concocted a devious plan. First thing in the morning, I would sneak out, retrieve the money, and replace it before mamma realized anything was wrong. It was perfect! It was glorious! I would live to see another day.

My eyes flew open early the next morning. I dressed in a frenzied blur, tiptoed past the

kitchen, and headed out the back door.
Mamma said, "Whoa! Where do you think
you're going? Get back in here and eat your
breakfast." Oh no!

With escalating anxiety, I sat to scarf down my
bacon and eggs. While sitting there, I watched
my plan disintegrate.

Mamma finished her grocery list and was
preparing to leave. Hurry! I had to hurry!
What would happen to me if she went to the
store and had no money to pay for the
groceries? I had to stop her!

While dreaming up a diversion, the words I
dreaded floated to my ears. Mamma said,
"There's forty dollars missing from my wallet.
I'm sure I had forty dollars in here yesterday."

Meekly, I lowered my head and continued to
eat. Silently, I listened as she systematically
questioned each and every child. Panic
bubbled and churned. Soon, I was the only
remaining possibility.

I learned a valuable lesson that day. Piracy is not a suitable profession for one prone to heebie-jeebies!

Soon after that, Robbie blazed his way into my backyard with a shiny, silver cap gun and an attitude. Cops and Robbers was the game du jour. We began after I sneaked into the house and, uh, "borrowed" my brother's toy rifle.

With Robbie in hot pursuit, I dove into bushes, climbed up trees, and taunted boldly, "You'll never get *me* copper!" Bullets flew and choking gun smoke filled the air. I was snagged by the hair and brought to the ground with a thud and a grunt. Busted!

The charges against me were resisting arrest and assaulting an officer of the law. Both were well founded, judging by the red marks on Robbie's arms and legs.

Exhaustedly, we flopped onto the sidewalk to rest for a while and decided to make some noise. A roll of red cap tape was just the ticket. We unwound the tape and hit it repeatedly with a rock. The resulting BANG,

BANG, BANG entertained us for at least half an hour.

Suddenly, I had a brainstorm. I said, "Hey Robbie. Let's go and hunt snakes." Since we were heavily armed and very brave, we wandered off into a wooded lot to bag an anaconda.

We hacked our way through the jungle with machete sticks, shot a lion, and ran in terror from a herd of marauding elephants. We swam with man-eating crocodiles and shot a headhunter or two. We struggled with flora and fauna from three different continents.

Mamma called our names from far across the savanna. We did not have permission for this little foray and were not anxious to return. We chose to ignore her. She called again in a tone that made it crystal clear that it was time to hotfoot it home.

We were snakeless, sweaty, dirty, eaten up with chiggers, and in trouble. Again! I don't know how Robbie spent the rest of his afternoon; I spent mine pouting in Sing Sing.

It did not take long, at all, for us to find yet another path to the woodshed. Robbie lived with his grandfather, who ran a medical practice out of his house. We were curious about the gadgets and gizmos that were in his office. We knew we were not supposed to go in there, but curiosity got the better of us.

Finding the office empty, we went in and locked the doors (there was a door on each end of the room that led to a hallway and the exit) behind us.

When Robbie's grandfather discovered that we were in his office, behind locked doors, he had a conniption. He was acutely aware of the dangerous medications and equipment inside. We were only playing with a percussion hammer and listening to each other's hearts with the stethoscope, but he had no way of knowing that.

You see, about a month before that, we had eaten an entire bottle of chewable vitamins!

He pounded on the door and ordered us to open it immediately. We were scared, and we refused. His tone of voice made it clear that we were in deep, *deep* doo-doo this time!

In desperation and fear, he sent word to my mother. Together, they alternately ordered and begged us to open the door. They threatened us and pleaded with us to no avail.

We huddled together and listened as Robbie's grandfather began taking the hinges off of the door. Knowing that they would soon be inside with us, we ran to the opposite door and waited.

As soon as one door was off of its hinges, we ran out the other door and streaked across the yard looking for a place to hide.

The adults yelled for us to stop, and we ran as fast as our little legs would pump. Unfortunately, they had longer legs. We were snatched.

After answering their questions about our activities inside the office, we prepared ourselves for what was surely to follow.

The inseparable, dynamic duo was, in fact, separated for the duration of the grounding (among other things). The glory days of the two musketeers were gone forever. Supervised play sessions were just not the same.

Chapter Five

Hurricane!

A grouchy old man once told me, "You're not a kid; you're a force of nature." After Hurricane Donna blew through, I knew that had to be an exaggeration.

Donna was my first hurricane. I could barely restrain myself in the face of so much excitement. Imagining the possibility of shrieking winds and pounding rains made me positively giddy. Yeah, this was going to be good!

Watching all of the pre-hurricane activity was almost as much fun as the storm itself. Mamma was a first-class planner and a world-class worrier. She devised a strategy to defend our troops against the assault with the efficiency of a general. There was a contingency plan and a checklist for everything.

We had our orders. We bleached plastic buckets and filled them with water; cooked and stored food; and stockpiled batteries, candles, and medicines. Baths were taken and laundry was washed. Windows were taped. Flyaway objects were secured.

When the storm finally hit, we were in a state of preparedness and ready to rest!

Donna slammed into the Florida Keys on September 10, 1960, as a Category IV hurricane. Winds gusted at 180 mph. Since we lived in Central Florida, the family breathed a collective sigh of relief believing that we had been spared.

Personally, I felt like Mother Nature had played a dirty trick. What a disappointment! All of that work was for nothing!

It didn't take long for Mother Nature and I to mend our relationship and become everlasting friends. Miracle of miracles, wonder of wonders, Donna skirted the Gulf Coast, turned to the northeast, and took dead aim on our little

town. Yahoo! We were in for a wild ride after
all.

Excitement was at fever pitch. I sat in front of
the living room window and watched with the
intensity of a begging dog. No one could
break my concentration, except mamma. She
dragged me to the table and forced me to eat.
The nerve!

Daddy was just as excited but made a point of
not acting like it. He listened to news bulletins
on the radio and attended last minute
preparations. He occasionally ambled to the
window to see what was happening outside.

Our little house was wood-framed and rested
on concrete, block columns. It was here that
we took refuge when the storm began to lash.
Our entire family huddled under the dining
room table in the center of the house. We lay
on pillows and blankets.

The assault began with 125mph winds. We
listened to the fury of nature's symphony. The
instruments played in percussion and wind.
Trees crashed, wind wailed, flying objects

slammed into walls, and rain pounded. The skies thundered and cracked with white-hot lightening. The house rattled and shook on its foundation.

Daddy held mamma. Mamma trembled and prayed. We children sat wide-eyed and listened.

It never occurred to me to be afraid. I wasn't old enough to realize that anything bad could happen as long as mamma and daddy were there. Oh, the faith and innocence of a little child!

When the eye of the hurricane passed over us, we went outside to look around. Stars twinkled brightly in the clear night sky. All was peaceful and calm. Oak trees lay crisscrossed around the house, and I was chest deep in tree limbs and debris. Mamma said snakes were probably everywhere and to be careful where I stepped. It was amazing!

We soon withdrew to our campsite, under the table, for round two. It was the same symphony, second movement. I fell asleep. Even a maniac has to sleep sometime.

We awoke the next morning to a scene of destruction, but our little house was spared. All in all, I would say we had a pretty good and pretty memorable time.

Chapter Six

Fran

The antithesis of Hurricane Donna was my big sister, Fran.

My earliest memory is that of her, standing by my crib, singing. "Froggie Went A-Courtin" was my favorite song. The verses went on and on forever. Uh-huh, Uh-huh.

Fran says I was as much her baby as mammas. I was her little doll to dress up, bathe, and feed. She morphed me into Cinderella or Sleeping Beauty with feather hats, costume jewelry, and discarded clothes. We rocked, read, sang, and played together, in harmony, most of the time.

In the role of big sister, everything was peachy; in the role of babysitter, everything turned to spoiled milk.

One night, mamma and daddy went out leaving Fran in charge. She wasn't allowed to spank us. We knew that and took full advantage at every opportunity.

After supper, a bath, and a story, it was time for bed. I didn't want to go bed and howled like a coyote. Despite all her efforts, there was nothing she could say, or do, to quiet me. I wanted out of bed, and that was that.

Finally, in total frustration, she warned me that she would cool me off with a pitcher of ice water if I did not pipe down and go to sleep.

What I lacked in obedience, I made up for in resolve. I howled with wild abandon, and she was as good as her word.

After the dousing, I thought it in my best interest to be quiet until mamma came home.

As soon as I heard the doorknob jiggle, I threw the mother of all fits. Well, that backfired. We both got into trouble. Fran was reprimanded for dousing me, and I was punished for not obeying her. There were no winners that night. Fran eventually forgave me but not until she got over being good and upset.

After forgiving me, she helped me learn a new game. When I first played Hide-and-Seek, I was like the foolish cat that drank forbidden milk with its eyes closed. He thought no one could see him and was always surprised when the stick fell on his head.

When the seeker began his count to twenty, I curled up into a ball, wherever I was, and closed my eyes. I thought he would never be able to find me. Eventually, I became upset and started to cry. I was always the first one found.

Fran was watching and intervened. She helped me hide. Once I understood the basics, I thought the game was really fun! Fran was like that. She taught me lots of big girl things that made my life better.

I thought Fran was just about the most beautiful girl in the whole world and loved to watch her apply makeup and fix her hair. Occasionally, she powdered my nose and put a dot of perfume behind my ears. I was always underfoot, when she dressed for a date, but I just couldn't help it.

One night, she wore a long, blue dress over a hoop skirt. A black, orchid corsage adorned her shoulder. It became abundantly clear that she could morph into Cinderella too.

We had strict orders, from my sister, to clear out when her date knocked at the door. She knew, only too well, what would happen if we were anywhere around. We would noisily kiss the backs of our hands, sigh, and make goo goo eyes until she was half embarrassed to death.

We also had strict orders to stay away from the windows when she returned. Otherwise, there would be three little sets of eyes peering out to watch her get a goodnight kiss. Bothers and sisters can be trying.

We can be *fun* too. Fran's collection of 45-RPM singles was our hot ticket to private concerts that rocked the house. "Monster Mash," "Ahab the Arab," and "Houndog" were all the rage.

We cranked up the volume, danced in front of the mirror, and sang into a cucumber. Shy was not a word that ever came to mind. Dancing was a no-no, but it was overlooked if we pranced around in our bedroom alone.

After a few twists, we invariably heard, "Turn that racket down!" We closed the door and adjusted the volume control millimeter by millimeter. The goals were to lower the volume just enough to pass parental scrutiny and to accomplish this quickly enough to prevent being shut down. It was an art.

We really aggravated mamma, but she did nice things for us anyway. One Easter, she made all of us girls matching dresses. They had lacy collars and satin sashes that tied in the back.

Fran was allowed to wear high heels because she was a big girl. Jeanne and I wore white socks with lacy edging and black, patent leather shoes.

We also sported bonnets that were trimmed with colorful flowers. We prissily twirled around and around.

Fran went away to college when I was only four years old. Memories of her are

Anita S. Sridharan

sentimental and treasured. She was my big
sister, my quasi mamma, and a good friend.

Chapter Seven

Tommy

Our family packed up and moved, to a retirement community, the same year that Fran left for college.

We rocked our new neighbors back on their heels. They weren't used to little kids and wanted peace and quiet.

Mamma worked double duty as a good will ambassador to the neighbors and as a law enforcement officer to her children. We were always kicking up a racket.

One noisy bundle of fun was a go-cart that my brother, Tommy, built out of plywood, an edger motor, and discarded wheels from a lawn mower. We steered by yanking left or right on a piece of wire that was twisted onto the front axel. With a good tail wind, it zipped down the road at about 25mph.

One morning, for a little extra excitement, I strapped on rusty, metal roller skates; tied a rope to the back of the go-cart; and held on.

Tommy took off, down the street, at full throttle. We were flying! I was crouched like a skier swishing down a mountain in full control. It was the most thrilling ride ever until disaster struck.

Tommy whipped around a corner, at the end of the block, causing me to slingshot into a drainage ditch at full speed. Wailing like a banshee, I examined my poor, scraped hands and knees.

When he saw I wasn't seriously injured and stopped laughing, I think he felt badly and took me home for some first aid. We laughed like hyenas after I was patched up and over my snit.

We didn't do *that* trick again, but we had fun with that old go-cart all summer.

Playing and fighting were equally amusing activities. My brother was good at both. He did anything and everything to pepper me up and enjoyed it immensely.

The most infuriating thing about him was that he ran like greased lightening. I could never catch him. When I gave chase, he ran ahead and waited until I got within a few feet of him. Then, he took off shouting, "You can't catch me. HA-HA!"

The best I could do was let loose with a verbal assault that would scald the feathers off a chicken. That seemed to please him greatly. The louder I yelled the harder he laughed.

Tommy may have been aggravating, but he was no squealer! When we did something rotten to him, he exacted his own brand of justice.

The problem was that we never new when it was coming. Somewhere, someday, and when you least expected it, BAM, you were nailed.

Returning from school one afternoon, I walked up the sidewalk with my arms piled full of textbooks. My brother sat quietly, on the roof, with a brown, paper bag filled with water balloons.

When I came into range, he launched a surprise attack, and I was deluged with watery missiles from above. It was a stunning assault.

I'm sure you are familiar with the expression, mad as a wet hen. Well, I was as mad, and as wet, as any old hen that ever clucked.

In retrospect, I really must give him credit. His plan was well thought out, well executed, and required a fair amount of effort. Bravo!

Another ill-advised plan required very little effort but was extremely effective in generating a high-intensity reaction.

Tommy slid under my bed and awaited my return from the shower. When I entered the bedroom, I was wrapped in a towel and very relaxed. It was nice while it lasted. He grabbed me by the ankles and shouted, "HAH!"

I was laid out in my frilly, blue Easter dress with white, lacy socks and black, patent leather shoes. I had died of a heart attack at the tender age of seven. Tommy was so sad! It was a recurring fantasy.

One time, he played a trick on me in the guise of sharing an experiment learned in Psychology. It was a demonstration of "coordinated motor skills."

He made a large cone out of newspaper and tucked it inside the front of my pants. Next, he handed me a penny. I was to close my eyes, place the penny on the end of my nose, and see if I could drop it into the cone.

With my eyes closed and the penny balanced on the end of my nose, I concentrated on the assignment. Tommy dumped an entire pitcher of ice water into the cone.

Hissy fit doesn't even come *close* to describing my reaction. Had I been bigger and able to catch him, I would have beaten the dirt out of him.

Failing that, I settled for calling him every name I could think of as I chased him around the yard. Of course, he taunted, "You can't catch me. HA-HA!"

With Tommy for a brother, I learned to always check under the covers before crawling into bed. I cuddled up with green snakes, cockroaches, fake vomit, and plastic dog poop before making the practice a nightly ritual. It is a practice I continue to this day!

For some reason, a lot of our mischief involved beds. Tommy had a set of bunk beds in his room. We made great forts by tucking blankets under the edges of the top mattress.

One day, we had the bright idea of playing bouncy baby. I climbed up onto the top bunk, and Tommy lay down in the bottom bunk. Using his feet, he bounced me up and down. The louder I laughed, the more he got into the spirit of it.

Eventually, the bouncing became so aggressive that the top bunk separated from the bottom and collapsed. I hung on for dear life and survived the crash without injury.

Our reaction was a mixture of twittering and worry. We tried to hoist the top bunk back into place before mamma saw it, but, alas, she was too quick for us.

With her help, we fixed the bed and noted another executive order. Mamma said, "Don't you ever, as long as you live, *ever* do that again!" We said, "Yes ma'am."

One of the things I liked best about Tommy was that he was generous with his time. If he found a treasure, he showed it to me. If he had a joke, he told it. He played cowboys and Indians, tag, and house with equal enthusiasm.

A whoopee cushion was one of the treasures that he purchased with his allowance. We experimented with it over and over on family members and ourselves. Watching how people reacted to the unexpected sound of PTTHHHHH, when they sat, never failed to bring us to a state of hysterical laughter.

Unrestrained laughter was all at Tommy's expense the day we went to the zoo. He was going through his meticulous phase, when it came to personal hygiene, and was very particular about having his own drinking cup. Heaven forbid he should catch our cooties. He would die of thirst before he would share a cup of water.

Tommy was standing about three feet away from a llama in the petting pen. Using a baby talk voice, he leaned forward and began telling him how ugly he was and how bad his breath smelled. It was as if the llama understood every word he said. He reared back and hocked a disgusting spray of slimy mucous right into my brother's face.

There was not a Kleenex, water fountain, or bathroom in sight. Daddy drove him to a gas station to wash his face. Poor kid! He took a real ribbing from me over that.

The payback was quick in coming. I was afraid of monsters, and my brother knew that. Sometimes, daddy had to check under the bed and in the closet before I went to sleep at night.

I believed everything would be ok if daddy signaled the all clear.

"Shock Theater" featured an old horror movie called "The Hand." In that movie, a disembodied hand crawled around strangling hapless victims. Every nerve in my body was on high alert when I went to bed that night.

As I lay there in the faint glow of a nightlight, I saw a hand crawling up over the edge of the mattress toward me. I let out a blood-and-thunder scream that brought everyone running. Mamma and daddy were not amused. That was one thrashing he couldn't outrun.

We liked movies and watched television whenever we could. TV's, at that time, were absolutely rudimentary. Following the initial warm-up, black-and-white images slowly emerged and filled our fourteen-inch screen. Tommy and I settled in, on a regular basis, to watch the thrilling adventures of "The Lone Ranger," "Zorro," and "Rin Tin Tin."

When the antenna was adjusted to the proper angle, the images were clear. When an airplane passed overhead, the images fuzzed, and the sound distorted to a frying hiss. Invariably, a plane whizzed by at the most exciting moments causing us to miss a climactic scene.

That was a source of great frustration and resulted in our jumping up to adjust the antenna. We shouted at the airplane, "Hurry, hurry!"

My favorite show was "Dr. Kildaire." I had a king-sized crush. It was worth a zap of static electricity to kiss his image on the screen.

"Ben Casey" came in a close second. The openings of that show captured my attention with their drama: "Man, Woman, Birth, Death, Infinity."

Tommy didn't like mushy stuff. I watched those shows with my sister, Jeanne.

Chapter Eight

Jeanne

Jeanne was the third child in our little menagerie. We were almost the same size and ran at the same speed. That enabled us tackle one another and pound until we were exhausted, finished, or mamma pulled us apart.

No issue was too trivial to launch us into full-scale war. We were as territorial as two little, fighting cocks and battled just as viciously. I provoked her; she provoked me; feathers flew.

We shared a room with one double bed. The headboard and footboard each held twelve vertical spindles. We counted those spindles to the middle, every night, and drew an imaginary line down the center of the mattress. That line demarcated our individual territories. We rested on our sides and face to face with noses, fists, and knees just inside the boundary.

Sooner or later, one of us crossed the line, and the games began. I accused her of drawing the line crooked; she accused me of deliberately crossing over.

We drew the line again and again, arguing more furiously with each and every encroachment of our space. Pretty soon, things degenerated into a fistfight.

When lying in such close proximity, one notices everything about ones bed partner. I drove my sister to distraction by singing songs in my head and puffing rhythmically through my nose. For example, "Jingle Bells" was puff, puff, puff—puff, puff, puff—puff, PUFF, puff, puff, puff.

After that, the foot wiggle jittered into play. When I realized that it was driving her crazy, I kept it up much longer than was absolutely necessary. In fact, I forced myself to stay awake just so I could needle her a little bit more.

Of course, she was an absolute angel! She wore curlers to bed, tossed and turned, and hogged the covers. She was way, *way* too bossy for me! I told her more than once, "You're not the boss of our bed!"

Sharing a bed with someone you feel warm and fuzzy about is far different from sharing a bed with a combatant. When it comes to things like digestive problems there is zero tolerance. We made no attempt, whatsoever, to spare one another's feelings.

One would think that two relatively bright children would eventually understand that fighting in this manner wasn't smart. It invariably led to a parental appearance and an unhappy conclusion. Night after night, it went on, and night after night, we were punished. Go figure!

We had a miniature, black poodle named Pierre who routinely went berserk during these and all other battles. He couldn't stand it. One morning, he did something so totally unexpected that fury turned to laughter in an instant.

Saturdays were chore days in our house.
Jeanne and I spent an entire morning trying to
clean up our room. We made the bed and tore
it up again a dozen times. We just could *not*
do it peaceably. I threw her clothes on the
floor and stomped on them. She tossed my
toys in the trash. We were awful!

The final straw snapped when Jeanne slapped a
wet mop around my legs. We were on the
floor, scrapping, when in walked mamma. She
had had enough and commenced teaching us a
lesson at the business end of a switch.

Pierre heard the commotion, raced into the
room, and bit my mother right in the behind.
Jeanne I looked at each other and burst into
laughter. Mamma stood there, in shock,
rubbing her bottom. Neither the dog nor we
scored any points that day, but we surely did
enjoy it.

What I did not enjoy was a dirty trick that
Jeanne played on me. Back in those days, we
had metal ice cube trays with a lever that
released the ice. Jeanne talked me into sticking
my tongue to the bottom of one of those trays.

I had no idea that my tongue would stick, but stick it did.

The screaming and crying ensued instantly. It felt like a hornet was on my tongue. Calling for mamma sounded something like, "YA-YA." It was best I could manage with a ten-inch piece of metal hanging from my mouth.

Jeanne stood by, helplessly, with no idea of how to help me. Attempts at pulling off the tray resulted in more pain and screaming. She heard mamma coming and flew, like a bullet, out the back door. She was no fool.

Mamma held my face under the water faucet releasing my tongue from its icy grip. She asked, "Why in the world would you do such a thing?" Since no one else was around, she assumed I dreamed this one up alone.

My tongue was beefy red and sore for the rest of the day. Since I couldn't eat, I was treated to chocolate milk and banana pudding. It was almost worth it.

We loved sweets. One of the few things upon which Jeanne and I agreed was that ice cream trucks were good things.

Upon hearing the first faint tinkle of bells, we scampered in earnest to collect pennies, nickels, and dimes. We tossed sofa cushions, checked under car seats, and shook piggy banks in a frantic scurry. This was an emergency! We needed to be on the curb, with coins in hand, before the truck passed our house.

If the truck was too close to allow time for a scavenger hunt, we ran shouting to mamma, jumping up and down, and begging for a quarter. Failure to procure the necessary change was a crisis of the greatest magnitude; success led to euphoric bliss.

Banana Popsicles were the favored treats followed by fudge bars, orange rockets, and chocolate dipped ice cream bars. Yes, all was right with the world.

Mamma had her reasons and wouldn't give me a quarter one day. I was absolutely determined to have one. So, I swiped a pair of pliers and twisted out a perfectly good front tooth. I knew that the tooth fairy would leave a quarter under my pillow.

Mamma took one look at my bloody mouth, the tooth in my hand, and gasped, "What have you done?" Followed by, "Didn't that hurt?" Of course it hurt; in fact, it hurt twice! I got a spanking to boot.

The Tooth Fairy apparently didn't care how the tooth got under my pillow. She honored our agreement and exchanged that tooth for a quarter. Thankfully, I had pulled a baby tooth and wouldn't have a permanent whole in my smile.

Jeanne and I slowly improved our behavior and gave mamma something to smile about. We didn't fight *all* of the time anymore; we just fought *most* of the time. Tetherball, badminton, and croquet kept us occupied with minimal conflict on many afternoons.

Monopoly, however, was a game that was eventually forbidden. It started friendly enough and invariably ended in a shouting match. We argued over rules, strategy, and anything else that we could dream up.

Jeanne wanted to trade properties; I didn't want to make a deal. She called me a moron; I called her a bully. She said no one would ever win; I told her I didn't care.

Our parents eventually tired of playing referee, and the game was relegated to their closet until we could learn to get along.

With a shortened list of options, we decided to climb an ear tree and play Tarzan. Jeanne was Tarzan. I was Cheetah. We got carried away with swinging from limb to limb. Poor Jeanne lost her grip and fell to the ground. I heard her arm snap from half way up the tree.

I never felt so sorry for her, or so remorseful, as I did watching daddy put my pale, crying sister into the car for a trip to the hospital. I couldn't be nice enough to her for about a week.

With Tommy away in college and Jeanne out of commission, I was pretty bored. Daddy provided me with a lovely diversion, one morning, and took me fishing.

We borrowed a small boat, with a trolling motor, from an old gentleman and good friend. Lake Howard was just across the street from his house, and a ramp provided easy entry for our cockcrow expedition. We launched in anticipation of a great catch and a tasty, fried fish dinner.

Daddy could smell fish beds and usually anchored us over a pretty good fishing hole. We tried several locations near the reeds, but the fish were just not biting.

By late morning I was hot, bored, and edgy. Needing to cool off, I cannonballed out of the boat. Since I could swim like a fish it was of little concern.

Imagine the shock of finding myself suddenly astride a submerged, agitated alligator! He viciously thrashed his tail and clawed at my thighs. I shot up like a rocket and broke the surface yelling, "HELP!"

Daddy had no idea what the fuss was about but could see that I was in a panic. He quickly extended his hand and yanked me into the boat.

As I offered a gasping explanation, we watched the surrounding water. A five-foot alligator soon popped to the surface about fifteen feet away.

Purple bruises and claws marks on my aching, inner thighs were my badge of courage and my proof. That alligator was the only thing I caught all day.

While Jeanne's arm healed, I entertained myself as best I could. I learned to ride a bicycle and enjoyed speeding around the neighborhood.

To this day I have no idea what possessed me, but I decided to race the garbage truck from stop to stop. It was a thrilling new race each and every time the truck went into motion.

On one particularly long run, I pulled ahead and looked back to see how much the gap had widened. That was a big mistake! I hit the curb at full speed, crashed into a mailbox, and knocked my silly self cuckoo!

The damage assessment read as follows: two bloody knees, two bloody elbows, one goose egg, one flat tire, and one crumpled wheel frame.

Great gorillas, I was lucky to be alive!

Once the bike was fixed and Jeanne had mended, we rode around, every evening, in a cloud of DDT. I'm serious. A pesticide truck, with a fogger mounted in the rear, passed through our neighborhood on a daily basis. Jeanne and I mounted our bikes, pedaled in close to the sprayer, and rode blind in the poisonous cloud.

In those days DDT was used to control the mosquito population and was considered harmless to humans. What was once fun is now a little scary.

In fact, a lot of the things we did are scary, in retrospect, but we survived and learned a lot along the way.

Eventually, we learned that being a tattletale was not in our best interest. We had enough dope on each other to make that practice extremely unwise. We knew how to keep a confidence.

Jeanne taught me to speak up for myself and fight my own battles. She taught me that fair fighting is not fatal to relationships. I learned that someone can love you very much and say, "I hate your guts," at the same time. Those were great life lessons.

Chapter Nine

Collective Mischief

The family that prays together stays together, and children who scheme together cooperate beautifully. Teamwork ruled when we put our heads together concocting illicit schemes. The fact that these schemes always backfired did little to discourage us.

Daddy and mamma went out, one night, about a week before Christmas. Imagine our delight at finding ourselves alone, with a mountain of beautifully wrapped presents, under a glittering tree. We gleefully realized that we did not have to wait until Christmas morning to see what treasures awaited us.

Now, how could we possibly get away with opening our packages early? Aha! There was a way.

Having sworn each other to secrecy by crossing our hearts and hoping to die, we collectively raided the tree. With the utmost patience and gentle hands, we slowly peeled back the tape on each and every package, taking care not to tear or wrinkle the paper.

After peeking inside, we painstakingly resealed the boxes and replaced them in exactly the same position under the tree. We even opened Santa's presents that were hidden in the closet.

Hah! We really pulled the wool over mamma and daddy's eyes that time, and we really ruined our Christmas. Feigned surprise took it out of us on Christmas morning. We went through the motions, but the magic was gone. We agreed to never do that again!

That year, Santa gave me pair of moon boots. They were platform shoes made out of two pieces of aluminum that housed giant springs. I strapped those on and jumped all over the neighborhood. Boing, boing, boing. It was so much fun!

Tommy was left in charge, on another night, when the folks went out. He told us scary stories to drive us out of the house. That way, we wouldn't pester him. Each and every time we harnessed our courage and came back inside, he leaped out of the coat closet or made spooky noises to frighten us away.

Eventually, we all got into a brawl in the living room and sent mother's brand new, ceramic lamp crashing to the floor. Mamma had saved green stamps, forever, toward the purchase of the lamp and was thrilled to finally have it. It now lay broken into a hundred pieces.

We stood in mute awe looking at the disaster. We knew we were *all* in for it this time.

Elmer's glue came to the rescue. We spent the next two hours gluing fragments back together with the patience of Job. We even filled in the cracks with extra glue. Since the lamp was white and the glue was white, it actually looked pretty good. Maybe, just maybe, mamma would not notice it. Hope floats. None of us realized that white glue dries clear. Oops!

Satisfied with a job well done, we settled in to watch TV and enjoy our Jiffy Pop.

The lamp was the first thing mamma saw when she walked through the front door. We were soon a pack of hangdog hounds. Heads dropped, feet shuffled, and the terrazzo floor received our undivided attention. We answered questions and proffered a lame defense.

Our expressed consensus of opinion was that we shouldn't be punished. After all, it was an accident, and we did our best to repair it. Mamma disagreed. Our bag of tricks was empty and our tear ducts were full. They didn't stay that way for very long.

We regrouped and agreed that we would try to do better. Yes, we were reformed children.

The next time, we wouldn't get caught!

Chapter Ten

Fighting and Fun

Fighting and fun flowed in and out of our play sessions so fluidly that we barely noticed the shifting tides. Conflict was in inherent part of play.

As a result we learned to negotiate differences, follow rules, and give the other guy a chance. Playmates were mirrors that reflected our own behavior. They gave as good as they got.

Backyard softball games lured kids in from every direction. Bases were made out of any available materials. First base was a sweater, second base a gardenia bush, third base a Frisbee, and home plate a boomerang.

All contenders for team captain formed a circle and played "One potato, two potatoes" until only two remained.

Next, the captains alternately selected from the gallery of eager observers until all were chosen. Everyone played.

"Eeny meeny miney moe" or the toss of a quarter determined who was first at bat. So far, so good. Let the game begin.

Two people gazing at one image often see it differently. When fifteen or more are looking, it can get downright dirty. Squabbles began within the first few pitches. Was it a strike or was it a ball? Was the catcher biased, blind, or simply mistaken? Should the pitcher throw a redo, or should the batter be given the benefit of doubt? Should little kids get extras chances?

In a worst case scenario, the pitcher reclaimed his ball and stomped off toward home. That would "teach" us. In a best case scenario, we argued and voted. Majority ruled.

Competition brought out the best and worse in each player. Little Miss Bossy found herself sitting in the dirt after being, uh, tagged. Mister Meanie Pants found himself brought down with a leg extension, compliments of Miss Innocent, the girl with big, Bambi eyes who was, oh, so sorry. By hook or by crook, the playing field was leveled. Inning by inning, players scored and settled scores. Adults didn't yell at coaches or tell us how to swing the bat. There *were* no coaches or groups of observing adults. There were only bunches of kids having good old-fashioned fun, figuring things out for themselves.

Combat was a game of our own design. The rules were simple: arm, hide, and ambush. Snipers lay in wait behind all available hedges and trees. Armament included water balloons, rubber band guns, sock balls, and palm tree berries.

Bushwhacked victims were startled into all out war. Most of them launched an immediate counter-attack. Friendly fire quickly turned these engagements into an every man for himself melee. We ran, launched, ducked, and dove until we exhaustedly called a truce and crumpled onto the battlefield.

Other victims ran away crying, "I'm gonna tell my mommy." Occasionally, they did tell. That usually led to a mommy-to-mommy conference and a general court-martial of the combatants.

We were all spoilsports sometimes, but we didn't like a snitch. Stomping off mad was A-OK. Running off to tell ones mommy was a surefire way to fall from grace.

Punishment for this offense was banishment from the playgroup until we decided we were good and ready to forgive. You either took your lumps like the rest of us, or you found somewhere else to play.

Kids always came back, eventually, and they came back a little wiser.

We found an old oil drum and added it to our list of amusements. Turned on its side, it made a great "log" that we could mount and roll all over the yard. We had a contest to see who could stay on it the longest. I don't remember who won, and it doesn't really matter. We had a wonderful time.

We made nightlights out of old fruit jars that were filled with fireflies and bug collections out of insects that were gassed with alcohol and pinned to cotton covered cardboard.

Everyone played Red Light-Green Light, Simon Says, and Tag. Little girls played jumping games like Hopscotch, clapping games like Kumalada Vista, and string games like Jacob's Ladder. We spun dizzily with arms extended, swapped bubble gum comics, and traded marbles. Motor Boat ruled.

Wouldn't it be great if life was still so simple? Wouldn't it be wonderful if we could fight, cry, call each other names, and remain best friends in spite of it all?

And, wouldn't it be grand if we could share, play, laugh, and find joy in the simplest of things the way we did when we were kids?

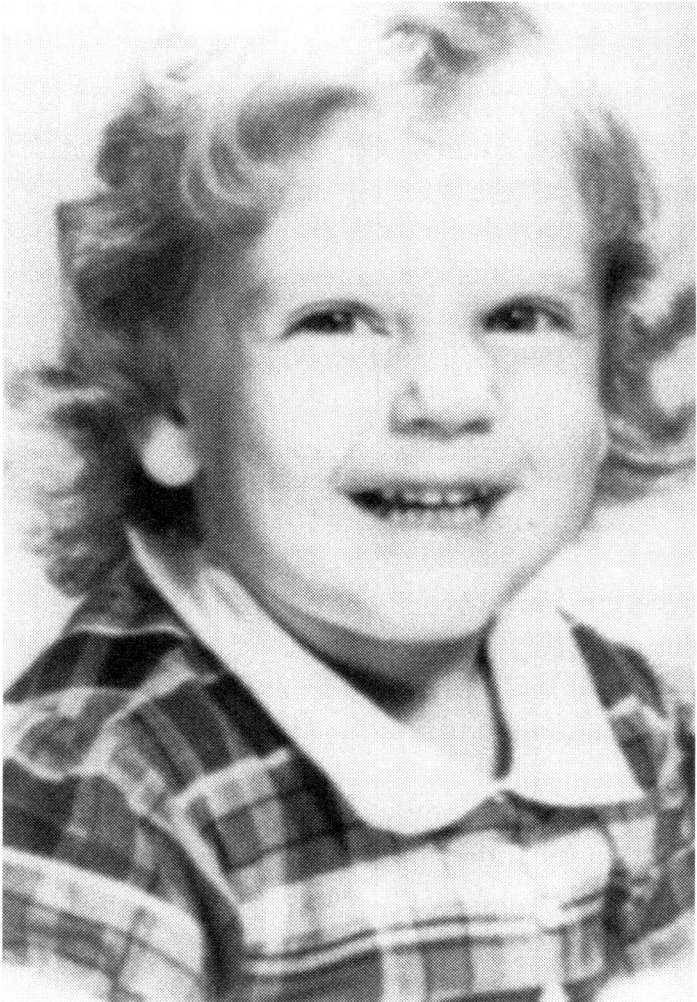

"The Baby" firecracker.
Susie at age 3.

back row: Mamma and Daddy
front row: Jeanne, Tommy, and Susie

"The Two Musketeers"
Robbie and Susie

Easter Sunday
Jeanne, Fran and Tommy
Susie in front

Fran morphs into Cinderella

"Tommy"

Susie. Notice the missing front tooth that she twisted
out with pliers for a quarter.

Susie and Jeanne

"Grandma Maggie"

"Mamma's Folks"
Grandmother and Granddaddy

Chapter Eleven

School Days

School was a very different kind of experience when we were young. There were, most assuredly, no classes in pottery or archery. Teachers pounded on academics. Exemplary behavior; "yes sir, no sir" respect; and our best academic effort were expected.

Mamma always told us that we would be punished at home in equal measure if we were ever punished in school. I believed her, and I behaved. A smart child does not sit up and beg for a double dose.

Teachers sent notes to mamma describing me as polite, neat, and a joy. She read those comments in astonishment and wondered if they were talking about the same little Susie that she knew. She once asked me why I couldn't behave like that at home. I shrugged my shoulders and said, "I don't know." But, I *did* know.

A kid can be good for only so long before something explodes. For me, that so long was the 7AM to 3PM I spent in school. After that, I had to let off some steam.

Everything about school was strict. Speaking was permitted only when a hand was raised and acknowledged by a teacher. Talking was not allowed on the bus or in the lunch line. Five-minute breaks, between classes, allowed for trips to the bathroom. We were expected to be in our seats, ready to work, when the bell rang and to remain in our seats, working, until it rang again in conclusion.

An infraction of these rules won an all expense paid trip to the hall for a paddling. Repeat offenders were sent to visit the principal. These were not social calls.

No wonder I was about ready to pop by the time I made it home. I made a beeline for the bedroom, tossed my books, shucked my dress, and proceeded to make noise, glorious noise, lots and lots of noise!

Mamma called me "the white tornado" because I raced around the house leaving a trail of litter behind me. She followed the path and sent me spinning in the opposite direction to pick things up and put them away.

She told me again and again, "If you would just put things away when you have them in your hand, we wouldn't have to go through this."

"A place for everything and everything in its place" was her motto. She said it until she "turned blue in the face."

Snacks, chores, and suppers were followed by homework. It seemed that every teacher labored under the delusion that he or she was the only one giving an assignment. It sometimes took *hours* to complete. When all of our homework was done, we were allowed to watch TV for a little while before going to bed.

God took me to task one morning when I was in the first grade and taught me a lesson about lying. Whether an act of God or mere coincidence, it impressed me.

I wanted to watch "I Love Lucy" and lied about having finished my homework. The next morning I awoke feeling fine but told mamma I was sick. You see, I didn't want to get into trouble, at school, for an incomplete assignment.

That morning I was a pitiable child. One hand rested on my forehead, and the other hand clutched my stomach. Oh, I was sick. I couldn't possibly go to school.

Mamma thought I looked fine and went for the thermometer. I expected an expeditious send off. To my complete shock, the thermometer recorded a temperature of 100.4F. I almost said, "You're kidding," and caught myself just in the nick of time. Instead, I said, "I told you so!"

Mamma put me on the couch in front of the TV. She bundled me up with a quilt and fed me chicken noodle soup. She even gave me

Aspergum. I loved the stuff! I couldn't believe it. This was *way* too good to be true.

The mercury continued to rise, all morning. By two o'clock in the afternoon, it read 102.6F. It was a raging case of tonsillitis, which led to a tonsillar abscess, and a trip to the doctor for an injection of Penicillin.

Soon, I was unable to swallow. I sat up in a chair all night, crying in pain, and drooling onto a towel. I was in undiluted misery.

The final result was one week of missed school, an avalanche of make-up assignments, and a commitment to never telling another lie as long as I lived.

A Christmas song admonishes children not to lie, because Santa will see. Forget Santa Claus! *God* will see! Coal in ones stocking pales in comparison to tonsillitis.

The following Monday morning, I was standing on the corner waiting for the school bus. I noticed that the rowdy kids were grouped together. They were obviously plotting something. We found out what that something was on the way to school.

The driver made a right hand turn and everyone jumped over to the right side of the bus. You see, they were trying to make the bus turn over onto its side. We *did* go up on two wheels. What happened next was ugly!

The bus driver stopped, stood, and bellowed. He was a stamping, snorting bull, and they had just given the ring in his nose a vicious twist. He was sore, and he was daring anyone to make a red flag so much as twitch.

The culprits cringed in fear as the bull lumbered down the aisle toward them. The rest of us watched in bug-eyed silence. He never touched them but sternly moved the ringleaders forward to seats directly behind him. He challenged them to move or make a single sound. They barely breathed.

When the bus came to a stop, in front of the school, the principal was summoned. The boys received a personal escort to his office where they were paddled and expelled on the spot.

There was no negotiation, no defense, and no appeal.

The rest of us, innocent and guilty alike, were treated to a severe lecture on the stupidity of our actions.

The school bus always fascinated me, and playing bus driver was a favored amusement. There was a vine-covered trellis that stood three feet away from our Florida room. The tunnel, created between the two, made a terrific school bus! An aluminum lawn chair served as the driver's seat, and an imaginary lever opened and closed the door.

I systematically shifted through gears and bossed around little kids, both real and imagined. mmmmMMMMM click, click - mmmMMMMM click, click. Who's that talking back there? That better not be candy I see! You're in big trouble, mister! You take your seat, right now!

Playtime was a thirty-minute recess that we looked forward to each and every day. Any threat of extra assignments, in lieu of playtime, resulted in immediate obedience in the classroom. Teachers engaged us in spirited games of Red Rover; Duck, Duck, Goose; and Kick Ball.

When we were too high-energy, they sent us off to run around the track. The track was little more than a dirt path around a stand of pine trees. That was where I had my first major encounter with a snake.

A four-foot long black snake zipped across the path and over my feet. Since I was running at full speed, I accidentally scooped it up with my foot. It quickly became entangled in my legs. Well, I just freaked! I was trying to get away from it, and it was trying to get away from me. As a result, we just about scared each other to death with our gyrations and desperate attempts to break free.

At last, the snake shook loose and slithered away. I lit out in the opposite direction, waving my arms, shouting the news, "SNAKE!"

Frantic teachers were trying to catch me, thinking that I had been bitten. Like Forrest Gump, I ran until I was finished.

Lunchtime was another break from classroom monotony. Lunch tickets were purchased every Monday morning and were redeemed daily in the cafeteria.

We were allowed to "visit quietly" as we ate. Monitors walked up and down between the rows of tables supervising our gastronomic merriment.

We frequently engaged in covert mischief and generally remained vigilant in watching for opportunities.

There was one little boy who blew milk bubbles out of his nose. It was his claim to fame.

The rest of us resorted to mundane tricks like turning our eyelids inside out or making disgusting faces.

One little girl played "pimple." She stuffed mashed potatoes into her cheeks and squeezed them out through pursed lips. She was nabbed by the ear and hauled away from the table. The rest of us, of course, nibbled angelically.

The next year I was transferred to a new school and walked back and forth every day. Once, I felt truly ill and wanted to call daddy. There was a pay phone on the corner, but I didn't have a dime.

A playmate told me that I could make a free call if I dialed the number and held the handset upside down. Since I was desperate, I tried it. Guess what? It worked! When I shouted into the earpiece, daddy could barely hear me, but it was good enough to get the message across.

I never tried that again. Maybe it was a fluke. Luck usually rode on my shoulder.

I recovered from the flu and returned to school in time for final exams. We all have embarrassing moments, and my most embarrassing moment in life happened at school.

There have been crazy fads for years. Valley girls, like, talk funny, ya know? Well, kids in our school fell into the habit of adding the es sound to the ends of words. For example, we carried bookses and wore shoeses.

During final exam week, I walked up to a cute, little boy I liked and asked, "So, how are your testes?" The second that came out of my mouth, I realized what I had done and just about died.

The look on his face said it all. We both turned into scarlet hunks of mortified flesh. I turned around and walked away. Later, when we met in the hall, we each looked the other way.

After that I was pretty content to keep my nose in the books and ignore the boys. Heaven forbid that I should embarrass myself again!

Before the days of copy machines, mimeographs rolled out freshly inked copies of test papers and handouts. Kids believed that smelling the ink made them high. I always wondered why everyone stuck the pages to their noses and inhaled deeply.

Did I mention that I was a very sheltered child? I was clueless and sniffed the pages because I liked eau de ink. I do not remember suffering any ill effects. However, I would not have known a "high" from a horseshoe.

School created many happy memories. We worked hard but found lots of ways to have fun. Success in school bolstered our self-esteem, stuffed our brains full of knowledge, and kept us out of mamma's hair for eight fabulous hours every day.

When all was said and done, school was a wonderful thing.

Chapter Twelve

Halloween

Halloween was one holiday that was right up our alley. We were *supposed* to dress up and behave mischievously.

Everyone got into the spirit of the holiday. Neighbors baked fresh cookies and other homemade goodies to give away. Children created imaginative costumes for themselves. Parents played along and sent their kids trick-or-treating without worry or fear.

Pranks and preparations began a few days ahead of schedule. There was a white, larger-than-life statue of a stallion on a business corner near our house. It was reared up on its hind legs, and its stallion's essence was shining out, in all of its glory, for the whole world to see. It was almost embarrassing.

Some little mischief-maker slipped out each and every Halloween and pinned a bed sheet diaper on him. It was typical of the harmless pranks that went on in those days.

Daddy rigged himself a costume that caused all of the little goblins to jump back and squeal. It was a pair of green goggles made out of two cups from a Styrofoam egg carton. He poked a hole in the center of each cup so he could see. It gave him the appearance of an alien with really weird looking eyes.

My costumes were put together from whatever I could find around the house. A few, gaudy baubles transformed me into a gypsy. An old sheet thrown over my head made me a ghost. Sheer scarves tied all around turned me into a fairy princess. Our ability to imagine was our only limitation. That was no limitation at all!

Armed with paper bags and flashlights, we were off. "Trick-or-Treat, smell my feet, give me something good to eat!" Of course, when we actually arrived at a front door, we sang out the traditional greeting and politely replied to the usual front door chatter: "Oh my, what a scary ghost you are!" or "Goodness, who are you supposed to be?"

Neighbors and friends generously doled out goodies by the hands full. We made out like bandits and raked in the loot. It was great!

We emptied our bags onto the living room floor at the end of the evening and sorted through our treasure trove of candy. We puckered up with pixie stix, sucked on Sugar Daddies, jammed with jawbreakers, and slurped flavored syrup from little, wax cola bottles.

We saved the rest for later. Mamma wrote our names on the bags and put them away. Apples, oranges, cookies, and brownies were taken to the kitchen to eat the next day.

We ran around the house on a sugar high and generally drove everyone crazy.

My Halloween spirit was dampened only once. It was the year I had a concussion. My costume was *good*, and I wanted to show it to one of my "grandmas" down the street. I excitedly jumped on my bicycle and raced toward her house.

Unfortunately, the hem of my costume caught in the chain, and I crashed onto the pavement. A passerby found me lying, unconscious, in the middle of the street and carried me home. Headache and nausea made trick-or-treating out of the question. Bummer!

My brother and sister shared their candy, and all was well. Of course, we *did* quibble over exactly which candies would be relinquished to me. Mamma settled the argument by blindly scooping candy out of their bags and handing it over. Case closed.

When all was said and done, Halloween was about the best time of the whole year. Neighbors had an opportunity to meet each other and give generously, children had hours of socializing and fun, and good-natured pranks exercised senses of humor. What was not to love about that?

Chapter Thirteen

Birds and Bees

Mamma was found in a cabbage patch. Daddy was found under a cow patty. I was hatched from an egg. Imagine that!

When it came to questions about the facts of life, Mamma's policy was to specifically answer what was asked. Like us, there were times when she was not eager to volunteer information.

In the beginning, I was satisfied with oblique answers. I asked, "Mommy, where did I come from?" She replied, "You came from God."

Pretty soon, I sensed mamma's discomfort and trotted off, independently, to track down the truth. I was as determined as a bloodhound scenting a trail.

A neighborhood kid told me the real deal about the mechanics of reproduction. I got mad and called her a "dirty, rotten liar." I knew my mommy and daddy would *never* do something like that. Still, it bothered me. Could it possibly be true?

With dictionary in hand, I loped off to the privacy of the bathroom in pursuit of facts. The definition of the word "intercourse" contained several other words that I did not know. Each of those words led to another definition, and another, and another.

About twenty-five words later, the answer was clear. My friend was right. Ha! The coon was treed, and I had no idea what to do next! So, I high-tailed it back to my friend's house barking and baying.

There are some things that a little kid just does *not* want to visualize. Heaven only knew what else I might find out! Ignorance was bliss! Purposefully, I took off scenting some other trail.

About the only time that I could catch mamma alone was in the car on the way to the grocery store. That's when I asked personal questions.

I once asked two questions that elicited a totally unexpected response.

Mamma turned as red as a beet, pulled out of traffic, and laughed, and laughed, and laughed. I thought she would "bust a gut." I sat in bemused puzzlement and waited. The questions seemed perfectly logical to me.

We had learned in health education that we began life as a fertilized egg. My only experience with eggs was with the ones we bought at the grocery store. I thought it must take a mighty big egg to hold a whole, entire baby!

In total sincerity I asked, "Once you lay the egg, how does the baby get out? Do you crack it open with a hammer?"

The second question was about fertilization. I knew of only one function for a certain part of the male anatomy and asked mamma if that particular function accomplished the job. If that was true, I was *never* going to get married!

I had more questions ready, but Mamma announced, "That's enough for today. We'll talk about this some other time." It seems mamma shared another characteristic with her children. She was skilled at the artful dodge.

Another question presented itself when my cousin came for a visit carrying twins. Her belly was enormous. She placed my hands in just the right spots, and I could feel the babies tumbling.

I asked, "Mamma? How are the babies going to get out?" She replied, "Through a hidden, secret place that God created." The obvious choice was the navel. I always wore a shirt, so it was a hidden, secret place. Also, it had no other function that I could identify. Eureka! I was *good*!

Just wait until my friend heard about this! I ran barking and baying back to her front door. She called me a doofus. Can you believe it? A *doofus*! The streetwise smart aleck gave me another word, and well, you know the routine. Egad! She was right again.

It seemed that no matter where I sniffed the trail led back to the tree. Even innocent snuffling in Sunday school got me into trouble.

One Sunday morning, our teacher was out with a bad cold. We had to go into a class with the bigger kids. Unfortunately, Jeanne was in that class. How was *I* supposed to know my question would embarrass her?

The passage under study was Genesis, Chapter 17, "The Covenant of Circumcision." In that passage, God instructs Abraham on the practice of circumcision. As innocently as a little lamb, I raised my hand and asked, "Mr. McGee, what is circumcision?"

Well, you would have thought I let off a stink bomb. Jeanne immediately dropped her head and examined her cuticles. The rest of the kids laughed. The teacher's jaw dropped, and he didn't know what to do. He said, "Uhhh…well …uhm…maybe you should ask your mother about that."

Since it was one hundred percent clear that I had committed a faux pas, I quickly agreed to do that and remained silent while everyone snickered and poked each other in the ribs. I knew I had stepped into a mess of some kind and couldn't *wait* to find out what it was!

After church, as soon as we were in the car, Jeanne lit into me. Mamma found herself in the hot seat as soon as Jeanne told her what I had done. Obviously, I needed some answers!

She began her oblique explanation about it being a ritual, and I would have none of it. I wanted *details*. If it caused such a gigantic reaction in Sunday school, I knew this was a good one!

Mamma said, "Daddy, why don't you explain it to her?" Daddy said, "No honey. You're doing a fine job. Go right on ahead."

Good grief! Won't somebody, *anybody* explain this to me? Poor mamma finally choked out the briefest possible explanation. Wow! I was right! Who would ever have imagined such a thing?

Now my interest was really peaked. I decided I might as well figure the whole thing out, once and for all.

Feeling as guilty as any little girl could, I sneaked a National Geographic and a flashlight into the closet and closed the door behind me. Since I had never seen a naked man, I needed to study on that a while. Pretty soon, I had the general idea.

Everything related to reproduction and anatomy was complicated! I ran back to the tree and barked viciously. That coon stayed treed for years!

Meanwhile, I was a happy hound dog out scenting on another one of life's mysterious trails.

Chapter Fourteen

Sanibel Island

Sanibel Island was the shelling capitol of the world and a beachgoers paradise. Our family spent sunburned days basking, fishing, swimming, and chasing away seagulls.

When enjoying picnics on the beach, we became unwilling participants in spirited games of "Dodge Bird." The object of the game was to defend against the diving seagulls that aggressively strafed our table with black and white scat bombs.

These tourist savvy birds had learned that a well-placed bomb resulted in ones plate going to the trash. They crowded in like noisy, scuffling vultures to enjoy our food.

The game was quite challenging and to the victors went the spoils. We filled our plates and ate hunched over them like Quasimodo's kids.

When the bombing became especially aggressive, we sought out any available shelter. Palm trees and beach towels, over our heads, offered partial relief from the assault.

We quickly learned that plate to mouth locomotion should be swift. If one paused to gesture with a potato chip in hand, those dirty little thieves swooped down and snatched it away.

Thelma was a family friend that joined us on one of those picnics. She was a feisty 60-year-old whose effervescent personality usually bubbled with vitality and good humor.

About half way through our frustrating meal, a second plop onto her plate drove her over the edge. She jumped to her feet and shook her fist in the air.

Though she did not actually swear at the birds, she performed a cutting edge recital of near miss slang. Stomping over to the trash bin, she deposited her plate a second time. She was grumping about "those stinking birds" in fits and starts all afternoon.

Warm, salt water baths in the Gulf of Mexico followed meals. Mamma's hard and fast rule was that water sports waited until after thirty minutes of meal digestion. Otherwise, we "might get a cramp and drown."

That was an odious rule for children who were eager to get on with it. We wheedled, and nagged, and watched the time until we could finally race across the sand and into the water. We shouted, "Last one in is a rotten egg!"

Rough surf with high waves was "fantabulous" fun. Jeanne taught me how to body surf. We caught a wave and rode it, faces down, until we were tumbled up onto the beach in a disoriented heap of arms and legs.

It didn't take long for my swimming suit to fill up with sand and tiny shell fragments that chaffed and felt icky.

Remember my streetwise, smart-aleck friend? She once explained the practice of skinny-dipping. I thought this would be a perfect time to try it. So, I paddled away from everyone and slithered out of my swimsuit. It felt glorious, but I was so paranoid about it that the pleasure was short-lived.

Clutching the swimsuit in a death grip, I began to fantasize about the report that would surely appear on the six-o'clock news. "The body of a little girl, who was naked as a jaybird, washed up on the shore of Sanibel Island today. She was apparently swimming nude and was attacked by sharks. Her swimsuit was found a short distance away."

Leaping lizards! I didn't want the whole world to see me naked! That swimsuit was on in a flash. Scanning the water for fins, I vigorously paddled to rejoin the crowd. Nope, I was not cut out to be a rebel.

Daddy usually fished on the pier while we swam. He watched us, and we watched him. I occasionally joined him to see what everyone was reeling in.

Ocean fishing was interesting. Each tug on the line heralded a mystery. What would be at the other end this time?

Daddy once caught fourteen fish on a single piece of bait. It's true! He reeled in a big fish and held it with his foot to remove the hook. Thirteen baby fish spewed out of its mouth. He won bragging rights, for years, with that tale.

When fishing was good, we ate whatever was caught that day. We built a fire on the sand, cleaned the fish, and cooked them on coals. My job was to gather driftwood for the fire. While daddy cleaned fish and tossed scraps to the birds, I searched for wood.

Scavenging the beach was no work at all. One found such amazing things. Clumps of seaweed, washed up critters, coconuts, and unusual shells caught my attention all along the way.

Snakes scared me nearly to death. The cosmos seemed to have some grand design for bringing us into close proximity with each other. There was a time when it seemed that everywhere I went and everything I did brought me nose to nose with a snake. Scavenging was no exception.

You have heard the expression; "I was so scared that I peed my pants." Well, if my swimsuit had not been wet already, it would have been anyway.

Reaching down for a stick, a jewel-toned wiggle caught my eye. A coral snake was exiting right, and I was exiting left. The load of wood I was carrying fell to the sand, and I was off. "Daddy, Daddy, SNAKE!"

About half way back to camp, I came to my senses and veered off into the water to rinse myself. Nobody was going to call *me* potty pants!

We enjoyed a meal of fresh "Whities" and settled in to digest. Digging in the sand for coquinas helped to pass the time. Coquinas are tiny clams with brightly colored shells. Holding them was like holding a rainbow.

We collected them and usually took them home. The shells opened, when boiled, and looked like little butterflies. We used them to decorate boxes and picture frames.

Once, I put a whole bucketful of these clams into the car and forgot about them. You can imagine how wonderfully everyone enjoyed the smell of rotten clams, on the ride home, two days later. It was not my finest hour.

Sunburned and sandy, relaxed and refreshed, we made our way home in a stinky car. Jeanne held her nose and said, "Gee, Susie, thanks a lot!" I stuck out my tongue and replied, "You're welcome!"

Chapter Fifteen

Critters

One cannot talk about growing up in the South without mentioning critters. They were everywhere. Warm winters and high humidity allowed populations to explode on a year-round basis.

Cockroaches were a fact of life. It did not matter how fastidious one was or how meticulously one cleaned the kitchen; there were roaches in the house. These are not the little roaches one sees in the northern states. These bugs are two inches long and can fly!

Have you heard of the happy dance where one joyfully twirls and kicks up his heels? We had a cockroach dance. This ritual was performed whenever we were in direct contact with a big one.

One night, I awoke to a tickling sensation on my leg under the covers. I reached down to

scratch the tickle and put my hand on top of, you guessed it, la cucaracha. The action looked like a flamenco dance gone wild. I whipped off the covers and leaped out of bed to squeal and jump up and down.
Olé.

Another time, I was in the shower, shampooing my hair, and felt something on my back. My eyes flew open in surprise and filled with soap. You haven't lived until you've showered with a cockroach on your back and soap in your eyes.

That performance was a Greek folk dance in fast forward. I whirled and twirled and eventually washed him down the drain with hot water.

Speaking of hot, let me introduce you to a nasty little critter called the Io Moth Caterpillar. These hairy, green bundles of fire can make a grown man pucker up and cry if they contact bare skin. Believe me; I know! One fell off of an ornamental and onto my shoulder resulting in a blistery, red patch of weeping dermatitis. I bawled for an hour.

Mamma put an ice pack on the spot and daddy squished the caterpillar with his shoe. He said, "Don't worry honey. He doesn't have the guts to do that again." Ha, Ha! Very funny.

Flies were everywhere, not to mention mosquitoes. The mosquitoes abounded in such large numbers that they could pick up a small child and carry him away. Honest!

There is no more annoying insect on the face of the earth than a mosquito who has joined you in bed. That high-pitched whine can drive a person crazy.

I eventually became an expert at reaching out in the dark and smashing them between my hands. It was as if I had a radar detection system. Bzzzzz-smack! Yes!

When returning home after dark, we gathered by the front door and counted. On the count of three, we all rushed inside and closed the door as quickly as possible. Otherwise, the house would be filled with the pesky little buggers, and we wouldn't get a wink of sleep.

Last but not least was the toad. Toads were everywhere after dark. We ran over them with the car by the dozens. Little toad pancakes lay all over the streets.

Toads used to gather around the dog's food bowl and eat the leftover chow. One evening, I made the mistake of walking out, in the dark and barefooted, onto the back porch. Yes, I stepped on one of the little suckers and squashed him flat. I had toad juice all over the bottom of my foot. Gross! I learned another life lesson. Always wear shoes outside after dark.

Chapter Sixteen

Mealtime

In spite of the fact that mamma put good and nutritious food on the table, meals at our house were always a struggle.

We had one unbreakable rule. Eat everything that is put on your plate. Mamma said, "Children in China are starving and would be glad to have this food." We must have heard that a thousand times.

Daddy was a meat and potatoes man who didn't like chicken, wasn't fond of vegetables, and couldn't stand the sight of broccoli.

Things turned tricky when those smelly green stalks were passed in his direction. All eyes fell upon him as he dutifully took a miniscule serving and dropped it onto his plate.

We waited with anticipation to see whether he could wiggle his way out of actually having to eat it. If he could get away with it, there was hope for us.

His most effective ploy was distraction. If he could open a window of opportunity, that broccoli would disappear from his plate and be forgotten by his children. Failing that, he would confess to being a bad example in that regard. If really pressed, he swallowed it down with a shot of milk.

Milk was a part of almost every meal. It was delivered fresh to our front door each and every morning. The glass bottle was hollowed in on both sides and sealed with a crimped, cardboard lid. It was my job to put the empty bottle on the front porch each night and carry in a new bottle each morning. I liked milk.

Liver and onions was a different matter. Once a week, it was the pièce de résistance and the bane of my existence. Night after night, I sat at the table until long after the food was cleared away and the dishes were washed. I wasn't going anywhere until I ate my dinner.

One night I had a brainstorm. Why hadn't I thought of it before? I diligently cut that liver up into little pieces, about the size of peas, and swallowed them like pills. Easy! I continued to sulk on liver night but left the table with everyone else from then on.

Our most infamous meal was one of turkey tails. Mamma, forever the bargain hunter, bought them "on sale" at the grocery. Their on sale status was no mystery to us.

Daddy offered the blessing, thanking God for the food we were about to eat. We were thankful for food, of course, but being thankful for *this* food was a pretty big stretch for me. I picked, pouted, and groused my way through it. I just could not get past what it was and what had passed through it. Yuk!

Turkey tails did not grace our table on any other occasion. There were some things that even mamma couldn't take.

Good manners were another source of devilment for little children. We heard at least one of the following phrases at every meal:

"Sit up straight. Chew with your mouth closed. Don't talk with food in your mouth. Keep your elbows off of the table." B-l-a-h, blah, blahblah, blah! Who invented manners anyway? What's wrong with little kids eating "like heathens"?

Eventually, we all got the hang of it and could be very polite when it suited our purpose. The problem was it rarely did. Good manners were for fancy meals. No? "All right, all right. I'll keep my elbows off the table!"

On one occasion, we were very polite and got into trouble anyway. We will never forget the day mamma's strawberry cake was ruined by a practical joke that took a wrong turn.

Someone, who shall remain nameless, emptied the sugar bowl and replaced its contents with salt. We drank sweet tea. It was assumed that we would all sweeten our tea out of the sugar bowl. It seemed a harmless enough prank. No one realized that mamma would use this sugar to sweeten a cake made for company.

Everyone was so polite that mamma didn't realize anything was wrong, until she joined us at the table and took a bite for herself.

After bidding our guests goodnight, a little detective work led to discovery, and discovery led to a three-name alarm. We scattered in every direction.

Chapter Seventeen

Church

Church is as simple and as complex as anything can possibly be. Personalities and preferences enter the church building along with their owners. Humans, even very good humans, are not perfect. It is a simple fact of life. Things get tricky.

Our father was "the preacher." He wore suits, delivered sermons, visited the sick, prayed for the troubled, and helped the needy. To us, he was just daddy.

Humor was a hallmark of daddy's disposition. He collected jokes, stories, and poems the way other people collected coins or stamps. If there was an atom of wit in anything, daddy could find it, store it away, and use it at some other appropriate time.

One day the doorbell rang and daddy went to answer it. When he opened the door, a lady from our church stood with her breast exposed and cradled a nursing baby.

It was one of the few times that I ever saw daddy completely buffaloed. He invited her in, called for mamma, and studied the floor. I don't believe he looked at her directly the whole time she was there. That was funny!

Mamma was a preacher's wife, a housewife, and a stay-at-home mom. She delivered meals to grieving families and taught Bible classes. She cooked and cleaned, sewed and mended, and rendered first aid. She nursed us through measles, mumps, and tonsillitis. Organization was her forte.

Sunday mornings were like the Firecracker 400 at our house. Getting a family of six members rousted and ready for Sunday school by nine o'clock was no small feat.

Daddy had a sure-fire way of getting sleepy children out of bed in a hurry. It worked far better than repetitious calling or scolding. He cranked up the old Victrola and popped on a 78-RPM recording of a nasal twanged nightmare about "rolling through an unfriendly world." We were awake and out of bed in a flash. It gave one real incentive to pop out at first call.

We shared one sink and one toilet. Since space was limited, we split up and rotated from breakfast table, to bathroom, to bedroom. Females removed pink foam rollers from Dippity Doo curls, while males shaved and splashed on English Leather. Girdles were hoisted, ties were knotted, and shoes were shined. Bibles, purses, coats, hats, and gloves were gathered in the final seconds as we sped out of the pit.

In our haste, we occasionally arrived at church in mismatched socks or shoes, but we arrived early and cheerfully greeted everyone we met. Good mood or bad, sunshine or rain, we did our best to be amiable.

Preacher's families live in a fishbowl and are compelled to be somewhat careful about appearances. It was a precarious balancing act and a challenge.

The expectation of perfection is both unrealistic and unfair. Most members had children of their own and were very understanding.

Daddy was once in the living room with the elders from our church. In the midst of a serious discussion, one dear child entered the room clutching a birth control device that had been discovered in the forbidden depths of a dresser drawer. "Daddy, what's this?"

Daddy handled the situation with as much dignity as he could muster. Kids have a way of keeping you humble. This was proven true on more than one occasion.

The next lesson in humility was taught to my mother, who was deeply embarrassed, the first Sunday I wore cotton training pants to church. Right in the middle of worship, my bladder let loose, and a flood of warm, yellow liquid began to flow across the wooden pew.

The people seated next to us didn't realize anything was wrong until they felt something warm soaking into their clothes. They raised the alarm, and people down the entire length of the pew began shifting forward to get out of the way.

I was still dribbling when Mamma carried me out of the auditorium at arm's length. Someone else jumped up and ran for paper towels.

Meanwhile, daddy was preaching away, watching this, and trying to figure out what the commotion was all about. Typically, he never missed a beat.

Some weeks later, another little darling tossed disappearing ink all over a lady wearing a white, linen suit. The poor woman didn't realize the ink would disappear when it dried.

We watched in horror as Mount Vesuvious began a controlled eruption. Boy oh boy, she was hot! Mamma offered appeasement and apology to no avail.

The ink dried, and the disgraced culprit humbly expressed regrets. From that day forward, she looked at our family with a somewhat skeptical eye. That was actually a little sad. We only played jokes on people we liked.

Mamma found herself in the hot seat once again, due to an apparent misunderstanding. One Sunday morning, just before services, I told a lady, "I can't sit with *you* anymore. My mamma says you're *crazy*!"

Services ended and confrontation began. Mamma explained that I wasn't feeling well and wanted to sit with her. She could offer no explanation as to why I would say such an outlandish thing. The lady countered by saying that I wouldn't make up something like that. It was an impasse.

Mamma "jerked a knot in my tail," and I held my ground. That seemed to further affirm the truth of my claim. Yep! That was my story and I was sticking to it. At the time, I believed it was true. Poor mamma. What was she to do?

We children were also the recipients of lessons in humility. Having your daddy in the pulpit, with an eagle's eye view, is a distinct disadvantage when you are misbehaving.

On occasion, daddy stopped mid-sentence, during a sermon, and gave us the stare down. We slowly became aware of the ominous silence and looked up to see daddy and half of the congregation looking in our direction.

On very rare occasions, daddy called one of us down during the service and told us to get up and go sit with mamma. All eyes followed our progress through the auditorium as we shifted locations. Thank goodness, that never happened to me.

Sometimes things happened that were not our fault. Anything unusual turned our giggle boxes completely over. One notable incident occurred when we children were all seated on the second pew from the front.

The Brother at the podium said, "Let us pray." The church fell silent, heads reverently bowed, and the kid sitting next to me accidentally let one rip. We're talking about a world class, big boy PTHHHHH!

We dropped our heads, crossed our arms, and tried our best to exert a little self-control. Our bodies shook with the effort of restraining laughter.

The fragrant wafting of an odoriferous cloud soon assaulted our nostrils. The worse it smelled the harder we laughed. Pretty soon, the entire bench shook with stifled hilarity, the culprits and our own.

It traveled through the auditorium like a wave. Anyone within earshot was quickly caught up in the comedy.

We all knew we had to get it together before the prayer was over. It would never do to have the whole church see us misbehave. About the time one of us got it together, someone else lost it, and we all broke up in another fit of giggles.

Eventually, we did recover by avoiding eye contact with anyone for the rest of the service. It was a technique we attempted to master over the years with varying degrees of success.

For some reason, things are always funnier in church. I suppose that is true because it is the last place that you would ever expect anything funny to happen and are caught completely off guard. Church is all about praise, worship, and prayer. No one anticipates an inopportune intrusion.

Once a little girl, who had not yet learned the art of cheerfully giving, fisted her quarter. When the collection plate passed by, her mother instructed her to relinquish the money. She began screaming at the top of her lungs. "No! That's my quarter. You gave it to me. NOOOOOO!"

About the funniest thing I ever saw was a baptism gone completely awry. Four variables combined to turn this normally joyous occasion into mass pandemonium:

Firstly, no one realized that a thin film of algae coated the walls and bottom of the baptistery. Warm summer days led to this unforeseen complication.

Secondly, the man being baptized could not swim.

Thirdly, he had applied lotion to his feet that morning.

Fourthly, wader pants become unbelievably heavy when filled with water.

The preacher entered the baptistery with decorum. The repentant man followed him. After taking a confession of faith, the preacher gently lowered him backward into the water.

At that moment, everything went horribly, alarmingly wrong. The man's feet slipped out from under him, and he went under taking the preacher down with him.

Panic set in, and he began to thrash. Lotion and algae joined forces against him. Arms waved, water splashed, and help was on the way. Men in the auditorium jumped to their feet and ran to assist.

Upon resurfacing, the first words out of his coughing, sputtering mouth were, "Preacher?

What in the Sam Hill are you trying to do, drown me?" He was assisted out of the baptistery leaving the preacher somewhat abashed.

A few moments later, the preacher foundered on the stairs leading out of the baptistery. The weight of the waders made it impossible for him to get out.

With that, the curtains closed. The entire congregation sat in stunned, amazed silence listening to covert attempts to assist him.

The truth may set *you* free, but it took two strong men to free the preacher.

One burly man at our church was Coach Carr. He taught our Sunday school class for several years. His booming voice and strict football coach mentality were in direct opposition to his fun loving, tail wagging, and puppy persona. He growled when we misbehaved and enthusiastically wiggled all over when he was happy. We were never quite sure whether to toss him a ball or a big, meaty bone.

What possessed us to pull a joke on him, I'll never know, but we did just that one Sunday morning. By prearrangement, we mispronounced every single word that we possibly could during text readings. Paul became Pay´-ool. James became Jam'-es. Normally literate students became stumbling, bumbling halfwits.

After a few minutes of frustrated correction, Coach Carr slammed his workbook down on the table and thundered, "What is *wrong* with you people?"

When we doubled over laughing, he knew he had been had. Yep! We got him good! It was the only time I have ever seen him completely at a loss for words.

The coach's deep, bass voice sounded good when we were singing. The music was a cappella. Voices blended together like coffee and cream. That is not to imply that we were necessarily good. Even coffee with cream can be lousy. Pure, true tones and ear jangling clinkers were equally heard by everyone. When we got it right, it was beautiful!

Before learning to read, I did my best to sing along. Sometimes my offerings were little more than heartfelt gibberish. I memorized lyrics but didn't always get them right. Everyone cracked up as I sang, with gusto, songs like, Bwinging in the Sheeps, Cavalry, and Twust and Obey. I thought I was doing a great job!

When it comes to worship, we enter with reverent expectation, hope for the best, and do the very best we can.

Daddy, would you crank up the Victrola once more, for old-times sake?

Chapter Eighteen

Grandma Maggie

Grandma Maggie was a hoot! She had a childlike gravitation toward naughtiness and looked for the humor in everything. We were kindred spirits. Maybe that is why I loved her so much. She made me laugh.

Grandma loved secrets and delighted in wiggling out any little tidbit of whisper news that she could tell. She was always fishing for something funny. I told her things that she could spread around and that I didn't have to worry about.

When I told her my idea about our hatching from an egg, she laughed and told a tale of her own.

There was this fellow that wanted a little mule. Someone gave him a coconut and told him that if he would take it home and sit on it he could hatch himself out a little mule. So, he took the coconut home and sat on it for several weeks. He even took it to bed with him at night to keep it warm. When it didn't hatch, he got mad and threw it up the hill onto a brush pile. A rabbit jumped out as the coconut burst and he said, 'Come back here little mule. Don't you know your mammy?'

Grandma sat on her front porch, one afternoon, watching Tommy and me quarrel in her front yard. She told me that, when she was young, she liked to fight with her brother too. Watching us brought back a lot of memories.

Then, she wanted to know what the argument was about. She told me not to be mad because I would look back on it and laugh. Of course, she was right. We sat companionably and chatted for a long time.

In typical grandma style, she never scolded or corrected outright. She slipped her training in through the side door on the back of a story.

Behind a cupped hand, I secretly grumped that mamma made us do a lot of chores, and I didn't like it too much.

She giggled and said, "I know just what you mean. Mother liked to have worked the tail off of me when I was little. I had to iron the white, linen table cloth so slick that, if a fly were to lite on it, it would fall down and break its neck. She was so clean she even put paper under the cuckoo clock."

I thought that was pretty funny and giggled too. She said not to worry about the work because I would, "learn to do a lot good things and make some lucky little fellow a right nice wife."

When telling her tales, Grandma laughed as loudly as anyone did. She told me all about the moonshine stills that used to dot the hillsides. She said, "We knew better than to go snooping around them places. You could get your head blowed off that way."

Whenever the revenuers came around, the party line rang out a series of longs and shorts, in code, to warn everyone. Bottles of freshly run moonshine were grabbed and hidden lickety-split.

One old boy hid his stash in bed with his wife, who was nursing a newborn baby. The revenuers never thought to look there.

Grandma could take the most mundane topics and made them dance and sparkle. She talked about outhouses and cranks, mules and chickens, dressing out hogs and baking pies. She took the best from every experience and carried it with her through life.

I love her and she loves me from her "good old West Virginia" mountain in the sky.

Chapter Nineteen

Mamma's Folks

Our family made frequent visits to see mamma's folks. Mamma was one among ten children. That meant we had eighteen uncles and aunts and more cousins than we could count.

More often than not, a fish fry at Taylor Park was the activity of the day. We ate hush puppies, coleslaw, and grits. Grandmother flash fried the mullet that granddaddy picked up fresh from the fishing boats.

After eating our fill, everyone scattered in different directions. The men played softball or football. The children scampered off to the playground. The women washed dishes and sat under a tree to watch.

Homemade ice cream and watermelon were the final treats before packing up and heading for home.

Overnight trips to grandmother's house always filled me with foreboding. I believed, with all of my heart, that it was haunted. No amount of reassuring or scolding could dissuade me from the notion that I would surely die of fright if we stayed past even one more midnight.

Eternal nights were spent, in shadowy darkness, on the living room sofa. I lay with the covers pulled up to my eyes in terror. I prayed and sang hymns in my head, all night, to survive and pass the time. Did I hear footsteps? What was that? I strained to listen, searched the empty room with saucer eyes, and stayed in the hot, cold sweat of panic until dawn.

As if I weren't frightened enough, the cuckoo clock, which was mounted on the wall over my head, banged open every hour on the hour and shouted, "cuckoo, cuckoo." I about jumped out of my skin every single time.

One very enjoyable activity for me, on these visits, was sitting at granddaddy's knee listening to stories. He tossed a few logs into the fireplace, lit his pipe, and regaled us with one yarn after another. We listened with rapt attention. Most of his stories were about hunting rabbits and quail. He was surely proud of his dogs!

When he tired of storytelling, he picked up his harmonica and played until he was out of breath. Sometimes, if I brought him a cup of coffee and asked sweetly, he played for a few more minutes before calling it a day.

Daddy occasionally joined in with his fiddle. It was good, old foot stomping, handclapping fun. Daddy knew mountain music. "Black Mountain Rag," "Bile Dat Cabbage Down," and "Turkey in the Straw" were some of our favorites.

Granddaddy was small in stature. A prominent trait of his Irish personality was the gift of blarney.

Defensive driving was not one of his strong suits. In spite of this, I never knew of his getting a traffic ticket. He was pulled over, on occasion, and successfully charmed the pants off of every officer he encountered. He did not argue or lie. What he *did* do was strike up a friendly conversation. Pretty soon, he and the policemen were laughing. Without fail, they let him off with a warning.

Trips to town, in granddaddy's Studebaker, routinely scared the bejabers out of me. He habitually turned left into oncoming traffic at busy intersections. I shouted, "Look out!" His reply of, "Don't worry; they'll wait," offered little comfort as I scrunched down in the seat and closed my eyes in anticipation of an impact. Horns blared and tires screeched.

It didn't take long to figure out why someone wisely named the passenger seat "the suicide seat." Each and every trip felt like a potential ride right straight up to the pearly gates.

Just past the gate, in the side yard, the citrus trees were granddaddy's pride and joy. He tended to and talked about them all of the time. We were warned not to eat the green oranges. They could give one a terrible stomachache.

Once in a while, I slipped out there anyway, salt shaker and paring knife in hand, to eat a few. It never bothered me. I was caught and chased away by the time I ate only one or two. They were surely good.

Grandmother was a big boned woman and far more serious minded. She was a no nonsense kind of gal. We tended to give her a wider berth.

Once in a blue moon, she told us a ghost story or two. Once in a blue moon was enough! Her stories scared me nearly to death! This was not the place to be listening to *that*!

One object of interest was the old clothes wringer that grandmother used on a daily basis. She let me help her on one occasion. Once was enough. She continuously scolded me about keeping my fingers away from the rollers.

It seems one pathetic girl didn't pay attention. Her arm was crushed as it passed through the machine and was mangled as it reversed its path to freedom.

That was probably not the best story to tell a little girl with a vivid imagination. The fascinating contraption was quickly transformed into a diabolical instrument of torture. From that day forward, I was pretty content to stand aside and watch.

We could always count on good food at grandmother's house. She put on quite a spread. Black-eyed peas, collard greens with ham hocks, fried chicken, and cornbread with pot liquor were standard fair. Most meals were capped off with vanilla ice cream and sweet potato pie. Yum, Yum! It seemed that visits usually began and ended with wonderful food.

Chapter Twenty

Family Vacation

Our most memorable and eventful vacation was the one we took to visit Fran in El Paso, Texas. In our wildest dreams, we never expected to take a trip to the west. It was a wonderful surprise.

We imagined how it would be to see cowboys and horses, cactus and dust storms, rugged mountains and the Rio Grande. Yee haw!

Daddy decided to drive, and we began our journey in high spirits and with great anticipation. We quickly discovered that road trips are an entirely different kind of vacation.

Jeanne and I grew restless and fought, like two tomcats, in the back seat of our Mercury Montego. We hissed, yowled, and took swipes at each other until daddy pulled over and asked, "Do I have come back there?" We emphatically answered, "No sir!" He most definitely, positively did *not* need to do that!

Faced with *that* proposition, we fought quietly by passing nasty notes back and forth and drawing ugly faces. We could still fight; we just had to be clever about it.

Jeanne and I collected change in a Ball Mason jar for several weeks prior to departure. Each and every time daddy stopped for gas, we grabbed our jar, high-tailed it to the bathroom, and headed for the soda machine. We had to work fast! Daddy filled the tank, and it was all systems go.

Daddy drank ice water from the thermos. Mamma sipped on cola and munched salted peanuts. Jeanne and I guzzled down an Orange Crush.

About five miles up the road, mamma began to yell, "Pull over, pull over, I'm gonna throw up!" She rolled down the car window and did just that about the time daddy rolled to a stop.

What was the problem? There was a gigantic cockroach, coated in syrup, at the bottom of her pop bottle. Gross! She alternately heaved, fussed, and gagged for the next fifty miles.

It was an eventful day for mamma. After lunch, we were driving on a lonely stretch of road that was flat out in the middle of nowhere. A car passed on the right. Once again, she began to shout, "Did you *see* that? I can't *believe* it! There was a big, old, bare butt stuck right out the window of that car."

Mamma was mooned. Turning a flaming red, she covered her face with her hands and stayed that way for quite a while. Jeanne and I smirked. We were familiar with mooning, but this was a whole new concept for mamma.

Once in El Paso, we were introduced to refried beans, mariachi music, and habanera chilies. The fire ants introduced themselves. I came to the conclusion that there wasn't much difference between habaneras and fire ants. Both could light you up like a Christmas tree, one on the inside and the other on the outside.

Come to think of it, there was *one* significant difference. Fire ants were not equipped with an afterburner.

One of the many places we visited on that trip was White Sands Missile Range. After climbing to the top of a silicon sand mountain, we repeatedly launched ourselves into the air to see how far down we could sail in one leap. We played King of the Mountain and engaged in all manner of horseplay. An enthusiastic sand fight left us filthy and pooped.

When it was time to leave, we shook the sand out of our hair and began a slow descent. I came up with the bright idea of running, at full speed, all the way to the bottom of the hill. I made it all the way to the bottom too, three fourths of it on my feet. I pitched face first into the sand and somersaulted, cartwheeled, and tumbled the rest of the way down. I had a scoured chin and a scuffed pride.

At last, our visit was over. We tried out our touristy Spanish with "Adios amigos" and began the long journey home. Daddy said,

"Do I need to come back there?" We replied, "No sir!"

We decided to venture off course for a tour of Carlsbad Caverns where mamma's sensibilities were assaulted, yet again. Bundled up in sweaters and jackets, we wandered through the cavern, sat in "absolute black" of the King's Chamber, and purchased souvenirs in the gift shop.

On the way up to the lobby, the elevator, which operated inside a 900-foot shaft, malfunctioned. It jerked to stop, slipped, and jerked to another stop. Lights flickered, and we caught a faint whiff of smoke. To top it off, no one answered the emergency phone on the other end.

We were packed in like sardines, and it quickly became hot and close inside. Mamma had a claustrophobic meltdown. She removed her jacket, peeled off her sweater, and unbuttoned half of her blouse. She fanned herself with one hand, put a death grip on my father's arm with the other, and proceeded to worry out loud.

That embarrassed me greatly. The longer we were trapped, the more frantic she grew.

It was with blessed relief that the elevator eventually rose to the top. Daddy was relieved because mamma freed her fingernails from his flesh. Mamma was relieved because she did not die. I was relieved to be away from an embarrassing situation.

We quickly exited to the parking lot only to discover that the car had been ransacked. My camera was stolen. Well, that was just icing on the cake. Let's go home!

Remember that lonely stretch of road that was flat out in the middle of nowhere? Our air conditioner chose this desolate place to exhale its last cool sigh and die. Daddy was aggravated and Mamma was agitated. Fuses were short and tempers were high.

Jeanne and I hunkered down in the back seat and stayed quiet. This was *not* the time to squabble. Even *we* were smart enough to figure that one out.

Home again, home again, jigitty jig. We reached the safety and comfort of home the following evening as weary travelers in need of a cool bath and a season of repose.

We did rest, and everything was soon back to normal. We were a simple preacher's family making our way through life.

Epilogue

Some years later, I ran into the old curmudgeon that called me a force of nature. He grudgingly waggled his head and said he guessed we turned out all right after all. That was high praise coming from him!

We have collected many memories over the years. Each individual has unique remembrances that are arranged in his or her particular way. A memory that is dusted and prominently displayed in one heart may sit neglected or forgotten in another.

Daddy is semi-retired. Mamma is still by his side. They have been together for sixty years.

We joyfully reunite, at every available opportunity, and sorrowfully separate our individual ways.

To this day, we navigate through life, full steam ahead, with a twinkle of mischief in our eyes and a hope of adventure in our hearts.

Life was, is, and forevermore shall be a
"Firecracker Frolic."

About the Author

Anita Sridharan is a registered nurse and homemaker. She was born and "reared" in Florida. After years of work and travel, she settled, with her husband, into the beautiful mountains of West Virginia to write on a full time basis. Although she has won awards in private writing competitions, this is her first published book and a labor of love. Her quick wit and keen insights blend into a delightful writing style that produces smiles and light-hearted fun.

www.ingramcontent.com/pod-product-compliance
Lightning Source LLC
LaVergne TN
LVHW011232080426
835509LV00005B/451